"Buy this book and read it carefully. Then buy one more and give it to your best friend and ask that person to do the same thing. I hope this book goes viral because it shows that there's lots of good news when it comes to the condition of the church in the West."

Scot McKnight
Karl A. Olsson Professor in Religious Studies,
North Park University

"Amid the widespread distorted, alarmist, and erroneous claims about American Christianity, it is always good to learn some basic reliable facts. Brad Wright pulls together a lot of good ones in these pages to reconnect people to reality. Let us hope that the misinformed critics and alarmists pay attention."

Christian Smith
Professor of Sociology, University of Notre Dame

"This is an extremely needed book that is a delight to read."

Rodney Stark
Distinguished Professor of the Social Sciences, Baylor University

"Brad Wright's book is well-written and intelligent, and does a fine job of challenging received wisdom on a wide variety of topics. I hope the book finds the audience it deserves."

Philip Jenkins
Penn State University and Baylor University

"A welcome, calming voice to the cacophony of data interpreters of American evangelicalism. Using insider sensitivity combined with a nose for objective data sources, Wright has offered evangelical Christians a real gift with this book. I hope they recognize it."

Mark Regnerus
Associate Professor of Sociology,
University of Texas at Austin
Author, *Forbidden Fruit: Sex and Religion
in the Lives of American Teenagers*

Christians Are
Hate-Filled Hypocrites
...and Other Lies
You've Been Told

Bradley R.E. Wright, PhD

BETHANYHOUSE
Minneapolis, Minnesota

Christians Are Hate-Filled Hypocrites . . . and Other Lies You've Been Told
Copyright © 2010
Bradley R. E. Wright

Cover design by Eric Walljasper

Published by Bethany House Publishers
11400 Hampshire Avenue South
Bloomington, Minnesota 55438

Bethany House Publishers is a division of
Baker Publishing Group, Grand Rapids, Michigan.

Printed in the United States of America

Library of Congress Cataloging-in-Publication Data

Wright, Bradley R. Entner.
    Christians are hate-filled hypocrites—and other lies you've been told : a sociologist shatters myths from the secular and christian media / Bradley R. E. Wright.
        p.   cm.
    Includes bibliographical references.
    Summary: "A research sociologist uses statistics to reveal the state of the Evangelical Church, showing that the church is in better shape than the secular and Christian media claims"—Provided by publisher.
        ISBN 978-0-7642-0746-4 (pbk. : alk. paper) 1. Evangelicalism—United States. 2. Christianity—United States. 3. Christianity—Controversial literature. 4. Mass media in religion—United States. I. Title.
    BR1642.U5W75   2010
    277.3'083—dc22

                                                                2010004334

To Cathryn

ACKNOWLEDGMENTS

I have many people to thank for supporting me in writing this book. Various sociologists and other researchers have kindly answered my queries when I was looking for information and data. These include Scott Thumma, Mike Hamilton, Roger Finke, Michael Hout, Eric Kauffman, Arnold Dashefsky, Mark Regnerus, and Alex Piquero. My thinking about this project, and just about any other that I do, has been strongly influenced by countless conversations with my friend and colleague David Weakliem.

The process leading to this book began when I started blogging, and I have Scot McKnight, Ben Dubow, and Chris Uggen to thank for that.

This book originally started off as a very different project, one that I worked on with my dear friend and fellow sociologist Mark Edwards. I appreciated and enjoyed working with him on it.

Various organizations were invaluable in providing data, including the Roper Center, the Gallup Organization, the Association of Religion Data Archives, the Inter-University Consortium for Political and Social Research, the University of Connecticut Population Center, and the Pew Foundation.

This book liberally borrows the ideas and data from prominent sociologists of religion and other researchers including Michael Hout, Robert Wuthnow, Mark Chaves, Mark Noll, David Olson,

Michael Bell, Eric Kauffman, Mark Regnerus, and, especially, Christian Smith and Rodney Stark. I thank them for bringing light to our understanding of religion in America.

Chip MacGregor has taken good care of me as my agent, and Andy McGuire, editor at Bethany House, pulled me out of the academic wilderness and pointed to many of the ideas in this book. He has encouraged and guided me through writing my first book, and he is clearly a better editor than I am an author.

I thank my friends and family for their personal support, including Vince Grier, Marc Fey, Ryan Bolger, Caragh O'Brien, Susie Carozza, John Wright, Freeman Wright, and members of my Bible study. I also thank my friends from high school. After all these years, you are still my reference group. (Though I should mention that my high school friends thought this book would be more interesting if it were about pirates).

Most of all, I thank my wife, Cathy, and my sons, Joshua and Gabriel. I don't know where I would be without you; I just know that I wouldn't want to be there.

CONTENTS

FOREWORD

"Why do you evangelicals love to make up and say such bad things about yourselves?" The question seemed quite off-topic. I was at the *Washington Post* building in DC to address a room filled with reporters with the Religion Newswriters Association. I was to give my thoughts on the differences between good research and bad research. But the question that came out of what felt like left field was actually quite appropriate.

For some reason, today's American Christians communicate a certain amount of angst about their circumstances. I wish this angst were self-focused criticism, based more on humility or self-deprecating humor. Everywhere I turn, it seems the sky is falling, and believers talk about the church like it's barely worth mentioning. While knowing our culture is wary of the church, we seem to, at times, take that doubt to extremes, far beyond what the real research shows.

To answer the question at the *Washington Post*, I gave a reasonable answer. Hopefully, it was a winsome defense of the church and the Christian's desire for humility. If asked the question today, my response might be a short "I don't know."

Each year, a new soul-seizing factoid that has no basis in truth circulates through the church and then through the culture at large.

- "Christianity will die out in this generation unless we do something now."
- "Only 4 percent of this generation is Christian."
- "Ninety-four percent of teenagers drop out of church, never to return again."

As Christians, we need to care about our reputation. Scripture teaches we will be known by our love. Throughout the centuries, the church has often stayed in the places others have fled, caring for the widow, the orphan, the hungry, the sick and suffering, earning a reputation of doing good and standing up for what is right.

In our modern day, the church answers the call after natural disasters, digs wells in Africa, and delivers the message of redemption across the globe. Those belonging to Christ should have the best reputation of any people in history. God's glory should be reflected in us, not the world's angst. We all know our reputation may be tarnished, but perhaps not as much as we might think.

Brad Wright calls us to leave behind the sensational, tabloid rhetoric. Let's hear and answer the call to ministry and missions that motivates the church to deliver the message of transformation to society. We need to reflect the values of God's kingdom every day—not wait for some impending day when we can finally show our "true colors."

I deal with statistics almost every day. What I've learned is that 68 percent of stats are made up on the spot. (I'm joking, in case you were wondering.) Seriously, I believe facts are our friends. But a misrepresentation of facts—even for the purpose of motivation—is damaging to our cause.

Rather than wallow in thoughts that we are despised, we should rejoice in the fact that we are given the ministry of reconciliation. When we live as those who have hope to distribute, we will witness the work of Christ transforming both the culture that puzzles us and the church we love.

It's true that some people don't like us, but probably not as many as you might have heard. Yes, there are some struggles, but not as many as you might have been led to believe. Either way, we need to get to work—armed with right information and biblical motivation. Brad Wright provides us with helpful direction to be well informed and to be about kingdom work.

Ed Stetzer, PhD
President, LifeWay Research

CHAPTER 1

Why Do We Hear
So Much Bad News
About Christianity?

Statistics are no substitute for judgment.
—*Henry Clay, Senator*

Some statistics are born bad—they aren't much good from the start because they are based on nothing more than guesses or dubious data. Other statistics mutate.
—*Joel Best, Sociologist*

Crying, "The sky is falling!" might sell books, but it never solves problems.
—*Ed Stetzer, LifeWay Research*

You may have heard the bad news about Christianity in America: The church is shrinking; Christians get divorced more than anyone else; non-Christians have a very low opinion of Christians; and on and on it goes. This disheartening news is often given to us in the form of statistics, which we seem to encounter everywhere. We find them in sermons, articles, books, and day-to-day conversation; and these numbers, based in research, seem official and trustworthy.

But there is a hitch.

Many of the statistics currently bandied about regarding the Christian faith in the United States are incomplete, inaccurate, and otherwise prone to emphasize the negative. Bad news has pushed aside the good news about the Good News.

A Questionable Statistic Mutates[1]

Let me give an example. I was browsing a Web site when I read a provocative headline: "Only prostitutes rank lower than evangelicals in terms of respect in the mind of the public." This didn't sound right to me, so I did some detective work to figure out where this statistic came from. Now, when I think of detective work, I think of the television show *CSI*, with flashlight beams in dark rooms, dramatic music, and maybe a bulletproof vest; but, alas, for me as a sociologist it's just sitting at my computer looking up data. Still, I found an interesting story about Christian statistics.

In 2002, the Barna Group conducted a survey of 270 non-Christians. They asked these non-Christians their impressions of eleven different groups in society, including born-again Christians, ministers, and Evangelicals. (I've summarized their findings in Figure 1.) The Barna Group found that born-again Christians and ministers scored high in respect, but Evangelicals scored rather low.

Figure 1: Non-Christians' Impressions of Various Social Groups

Social group	Favorable	In-Between	Unfavorable	Don't Know
Military officers	56%	32%	6%	6%
Ministers	44%	40%	9%	7%
Born-again Christians	32%	41%	17%	10%
Democrats	32%	47%	12%	9%

Real estate agents	30%	51%	11%	8%
Movie & TV actors	25%	54%	14%	7%
Lawyers	24%	53%	18%	5%
Republicans	23%	47%	22%	8%
Lesbians	23%	38%	30%	11%
Evangelicals	22%	33%	23%	22%
Prostitutes	5%	29%	55%	11%

Source: The Barna Group, 2002

Based on these data, the Barna Group concluded that non-Christians are "dismissive" of Evangelicals. According to the article, this negative opinion has consequences: "One reason why evangelical churches across the nation are not growing is due to the image that non-Christian adults have of evangelical individuals." Wow, if this is true, it gives us a key to church growth—changing non-Christians' negative impressions of Christians.

But frankly, I'm not sure how much credence we should give to the Barna Group's conclusion, for several reasons. I'm going to go into a bit of detail about this statistic, not necessarily because it is so important in its own right, but rather to illustrate that we can't always believe every statistic we hear.

To start with, I wonder if there was some confusion among the respondents. Notice the unusually high number who were unsure of their response to Evangelicals, answering with a "don't know." This number was twice as high as it was for any other category. The reason for this confusion may have been that the question appears to have been worded peculiarly, for it asked about Evangelicals, not evangelical Christians. Perhaps some respondents thought the survey was asking about evangelists—the people who knock at your door when you're just sitting down for dinner.[2]

When the Barna Group asked specifically about born-again Christians, the respondents were much more favorable, ranking them third highest overall. How many of us, Christian or otherwise, could describe the difference between a born-again Christian and an Evangelical? Some surveys have even used the terms interchangeably, so the fact that the Barna Group's study found such different results for these two groups raises a red flag.

The second reason I'm skeptical of the Barna Group's conclusion has to do with math, so bear with me for a moment. The Barna Group's discussion of this statistic focuses on the fact that only 23% of respondents had a favorable impression of Evangelicals. This number, however, includes the respondents who "don't know" in the denominator. In other words, if you asked the question "Twenty-three percent of what?" the answer would be "Twenty-three percent of the 270 people who took the survey." But this isn't quite fair. It would make more sense to answer the question "How many people have a favorable impression among those who have heard of Evangelicals in the first place?" After all, if you don't know what an Evangelical is, there's no chance of having a good impression of them. Dropping the "don't know" respondents from the denominator bumps the number of favorable ratings of Evangelicals to 28% (23/(23+33+22). This puts Evangelicals in the middle of Figure 1 (even when you do the same to the other groups).

There is also a problem related to the sample size of only 270 survey participants. There is nothing wrong with smaller studies, per se, but the smaller size just means that we can only detect big differences between groups, and not small ones, such as those found in Figure 1. Looking at the data, my guess is that there is no meaningful (i.e., statistically significant) difference between actors, lawyers, Republicans, lesbians, and Evangelicals, for they each have 23 to 25% favorable ratings. With this small sample size, the study gives no evidence that these groups are statistically different (in terms of favorability) in the general population.

Finally, even if we accept that this statistic accurately reflects public opinion (which, as will be discussed in chapter 8, it probably doesn't), the picture it paints isn't all that bad. Less than 1 in 4 (23%) of the non-Christian respondents held unfavorable opinions about Evangelicals. The rest were either positive, of no opinion, or didn't know. This seems to be a reasonably low number, given that none of the respondents embraced the tenets of Christianity.

My take on these data is that they certainly should be viewed with caution, and they may even demonstrate a positive view of Christians. If a student turned this in for a class assignment, I would tell him that he has an interesting research question, but he should redo his analyses and presentation. However, the Barna Group's findings and conclusion were catchy, so they were picked up by the media. *The Atlantic* magazine (July 2003) summarized this study with the title "Evangelicals and Prostitutes." They wrote that "Non-Christians, it turns out, have a low regard for evangelical Christians, whom they view less favorably than all the above-mentioned groups except one: prostitutes."

Christine Wicker, in her book *The Fall of the Evangelical Nation: The Surprising Crisis Inside the Church,* summarized the study as follows: "When asked to rate eleven groups in terms of respect, non-Christians rated Evangelicals tenth. Only prostitutes rated lower" (143). She did not even cite the original study, instead presenting it as an unambiguous fact reflecting high "anti-evangelical sentiment."

From Wicker's book, a Christian organization named Off the Map picked up the statistic and featured it on their Web site as evidence that Christianity is losing its influence in America.[3] On the same Web page, they also advertised registration for their conferences that teach attendees how to reverse this trend.

From the Off the Map Web site, several bloggers found the statistic and put their own spin on it. One Web site, "A Blind Beggar" (subtitled "Devoted to the Journey of Christianity"), summarized it as "Only prostitutes rank lower than evangelicals in terms of respect in the mind of the public."[4] Notice that now Evangelicals are disrespected by society as a whole, not just non-Christians. Another Web site recast the statistic as "Only prostitutes rank lower than Evangelicals." [5] Forget respect, Evangelicals are lower in everything. The Barna Group's statistic was not particularly well-constructed to begin with, but it got substantially less accurate and more dire with each retelling.

The Social Forces That Shape Christian Statistics

The thesis of this book is that Christians are exposed to many inaccurate statistics about our faith. To understand why this happens, we should look at how these statistics are produced and how they spread through the public. Thousands of statistics are generated each year, but we only hear a few of them. Why do we hear these particular ones? [6]

You might think that only the most accurate and important statistics see the light of day, and so we can trust what we hear. Ah, wouldn't that be nice. In fact, if you believe this, I should probably also tell you that politicians don't always keep their promises, television advertisements exaggerate their products, and investment opportunities in spam e-mails are rip-offs. (The Easter Bunny may not be real either—I'm still looking into that one.)

The fact is, statistical research is an inherently messy and thoroughly human activity. Research findings reflect insight, error, and self-interest. People make statistics, and like everything else that people make, the results are mixed. Some statistics are good, some are bad, and a lot are in between.

Let's start with the person who makes the statistic. Some statistics about Christianity come from academic researchers such as university professors. We (and I am one of them) hopefully use rigorous research methods, and we have peers anonymously review our work as a form of quality control. Unfortunately, we usually write in highly technical language, and we publish in obscure academic journals. Also, we tend to choose topics that have little relevance to the day-to-day workings of Christianity, so we're often irrelevant to the church. Furthermore, most academics are liberal and relatively few are Christians, so an antireligious, or at least irreligious, bias can permeate academic research on religion.

Other sources of statistics include Christian research organizations such as the Barna Group, LifeWay Research, Reveal, and Open Tomb, as well as denominational research groups. These organizations do practical research for Christians—exploring issues that really matter to the church. They are headed by believers, so they share the worldview of Christian readers. They also do a good job presenting their findings in an accessible manner. Unfortunately, the quality of their work varies widely. Some of the researchers are not formally trained in social research, and they almost never submit their work to a peer-review process, so there's no external quality check. These groups are usually self-funded, so they may produce research with an eye on the bottom line. This may provide a hard-to-resist incentive to highlight "provocative" findings that will increase sales of reports and books and services. Unfortunately, these provocative findings are often those that cast Christianity in a negative light.

Still other research comes from in-house studies by various Christian groups. A church might study its members, or a magazine may survey its readers. Here the research is highly relevant to the group collecting it, but its quality is usually unknown. It is also difficult to know whether the findings from these in-house studies apply to anybody outside that particular group.

Also, sometimes Christian leaders will express their opinions and experiences in statistical terms, and these become accepted as facts. For example, a well-known Christian apologist has been quoted as saying that in his observation, evangelical youth are only about 10% less likely to engage in premarital sex than non-Evangelicals.[7]

We trust these numbers because we trust the person, but in reality the numbers are probably made up.

In addition to academic and Christian sources, Christian leaders get statistical information from as wide a variety of sources as anyone else in society. These include the U.S. Census, government reports, and survey organizations such as Gallup, media surveys, and political think tanks. Some of these sources, such as think tanks, will have their own biases. Media studies are often done quickly, to catch the latest news cycle, and so they may suffer in quality. Others, such as the better-known survey organizations, go to great lengths to accurately describe the population, but they still have an incentive to highlight the more provocative findings. Their surveys are often funded by other organizations, so their survey topics and questions might reflect the interests of the funding organization.

While many, many statistics are created about Christianity, most slip quietly into the numeric afterlife and nobody ever hears of them. Some, however, receive wide exposure in both the Christian church and the media, and both the church and the media tend to select and pass along statistics that reflect bad news about Christianity. It probably doesn't surprise you that the media may want to emphasize the negative, but why would Christian leaders and teachers do the same? Wouldn't they want to make Christianity look as good as possible?

Christian pastors, teachers, and other leaders often use statistics to highlight the severity of a problem, either with society as a whole or with Christians in particular. For example, if an author is writing a book on sexual purity for Christians, he will probably start with statistics about how impure Christians are, thus demonstrating the need for his book. Or if a pastor is teaching on the importance of tithing, she might first look for statistics highlighting how few Christians tithe, and then use these numbers to motivate her listeners to give more. With the best of intentions, Christians sometimes pick statistics for their usefulness rather than for accuracy, and the most useful statistics are often those that cast the church in a negative light.

Meanwhile, the mainstream media favors statistics that are newsworthy. Newsworthiness to the media usually means "unexpected" or "ironic" or "tragic." For example, one airplane crashing is headline news, but the thousands that land safely each day are not. When it comes to religion in general, and Christianity in particular, newsworthy stories are often those that highlight religious people not living up to their moral code, and so frequently we hear of Christians' moral failings. In a city with hundreds of pastors, for instance, suppose that almost every single one lives a holy life of loving and serving others, but one is found passed out in a shopping cart in front of a strip club. Guess which pastor will be on the front page? It's not that the media is necessarily biased against Christianity (the evidence on that is mixed). Rather, it wants to sell newspapers and airtime, and so it selects stories and facts to this end. For Christianity, this means a lot of negative stories.

Perhaps nowhere is the selective representation of Christians more apparent than with Catholic priests. Historian Phillip Jenkins reviews common portrayals of clergy in film and television, and, well, if you see a priest on screen, you know that something bad is going to happen. Among the plotlines reviewed by Jenkins: priests living sexually promiscuous lifestyles, priests systematically raping children, Catholic organizations condoning murder, and a satanic cardinal. Jenkins summarizes: "Somewhere in the 1980s, Hollywood decided that senior Catholic clerics made reliable stock villains, as predictably evil as corporate executives or drug kingpins."[8] He makes the case that other social groups receive far better treatment. "No studio would contemplate making a film that would be deemed offensive by (for example) Blacks or Native Americans," but "Catholics (and perhaps Evangelicals)" are not afforded this dignity.[9]

Once a statistic is introduced to the Christian church, another dynamic comes into play. As people tell the statistic to others, they sometimes misquote or misremember. The statistics described above about Evangelicals and prostitutes demonstrate how this works. This process is akin to the telephone game that elementary schoolteachers use to teach the dangers of gossip. As kids sit in a circle, the teacher gives a message to the first student, who then whispers it to the next student, and so on until the message has gone full-circle. Invariably the message is quite different in the end. What starts off as "Have a nice day" can end up as "Free Paraguay now!" Paradoxically, with each retelling, not only does a statistic move toward less accuracy, it also becomes more believable because more people have heard it. If we hear a fact from enough different sources, then of course we believe it, and even inaccurate facts can become enshrined as cultural myths.

The High Cost of Negative Statistics

I write this not to criticize researchers, teachers, and the media as doing wrong, per se, for they are simply being influenced by incentives and opportunities. Rather, I want to highlight the problems caused for the church by the continuing emphasis on negatively slanted statistics. It can be demoralizing for Christians to constantly read and hear about how the church is failing, and this in turn can undercut the church's efforts to mobilize its followers. Why should Christians give their all to God's work in churches if churches are failures? The effect is similar to that of stories about plane crashes. Just as the media's emphasis on plane accidents rather than plane safety can make some people afraid to fly, constant bad news about Christianity can lessen our desire and efforts to participate in it.

This bad news might also diminish evangelism. If Christians think ill of their faith, why would they want to invite their non-believing friends to participate in it? We invite our friends to good restaurants, not bad ones; interesting movies, not boring ones; so why would we want to bring others into a church that is portrayed as ineffective and sinful? Furthermore, non-Christians, as they too hear the bad news about Christianity, understandably would be less inclined to take it seriously.

Another problem of hearing so much inaccurate bad news is that it can distract from what really is bad news. If too many books and articles and sermons seek to motivate Christians with bad news, we can become immune to it. Then when real bad news comes along, we might not respond appropriately. Imagine a boy in a fairy tale who constantly cites statistics about the increased rates of wolves in an area even when they aren't true. Then when the wolf rates actually increase, who would believe him?

Finally, one last problem I want to highlight is in regard to the nature of fear as motivation. This is a question perhaps best answered by psychologists or theologians, but it seems to me that fear is not a suitable, long-lasting motivator for doing the right thing. I can't imagine that it has enduring, beneficial effects. Not only does fear wear off rather quickly, but it can result in self-protection and anxiety rather than in reaching out to others. I'm not arguing that we ignore legitimate bad news. Rather, I'm saying that routinely using fear to motivate, while it may be a relatively easy approach, may not be particularly effective.

There is no shortage of irony here. Christian teachers and leaders might focus on the failures of the church to motivate their members to do better; but in taking a negative approach, they might actually hinder the success of the church. These well-intentioned efforts might do more harm than good. Just imagine if we used this kind of fear appeal in our everyday lives. Let's say that you didn't like your wife's cooking. You could say, "Honey, tonight you served us jarringly inedible tofu, again, and if this continues, we will cease to function as a family unit. However, I have truly good news, for I have prepared a series of menus centered on steak and pork chops."

How do we recognize fear appeals? They often have three components: a strong adjective (or adverb), a dire prediction, and an upbeat remedy. Some of the adjectives that I've read include *startling, sobering, jarring, alarming,* and *dangerous.* The dire predictions include "the coming crisis," "an epidemic," "this will be the last generation," "the church in crisis," "the coming collapse of Christianity," and "the deterioration of our faith." The proposed remedies are often introduced with language like "optimistic," "provides hope," "we can correct and rebuild," "follow our biblical blueprint," and "rebuild and restore the church."

In writing this, I realize that I may have made a strategic error in discussing why I have written this book: I have neglected to add a fear appeal. So maybe no one will read it. But it's not too late, so here it goes. You should read this book because "there is a deeply disturbing trend of bad statistics that is sabotaging American Christianity and destroying the American way of life, and if you ignore it your entire body will soon be covered with boils. The good news, however, is that if you buy this book and read it carefully, you will avoid this calamity; plus you'll live longer, have fresh breath, and your kitchen knives will always stay sharp."

Getting It Right

This book is not about ignoring bad news to focus solely on good news. Overemphasizing the good news has its own problems, and the church would do best by looking at itself honestly. It is also not a refutation of the value of statistics to the church. The fact that statistics are socially influenced simply means that we need to understand how they come to be, not reject them outright. I'm a card-carrying quantitative sociologist, and I really like statistics. If nothing else, it's probably much easier to lie without statistics than to lie with them.

The purpose of this book is rather simple. Using the best available data, I will describe how Christians are doing in six areas: church growth, what we believe, our participation in church activities, family and sexual issues, how we treat others, and how others see us. In each of these areas, there are various myths floating around about American Christianity, and I want to examine if these myths are true. In a sense, this book is like the popular television show *Myth-Busters*, on which they test everyday assumptions about how things work. Unfortunately, I don't get to blow things up—a mainstay on the show—but I do get to present a lot of data.

My goal is not to show the church in a particular light but rather to let the data speak for themselves. Having said that, the answers provided here provide some surprisingly good news for Christians.

This book focuses on Evangelical Christians because as an Evangelical Christian myself, this is my vantage point in looking at these issues. As such, I am aware of the many myths perpetrated about Evangelicals. But the analyses include Mainline Protestants and Catholics as well, and so many of the ideas in this book apply to American Christianity more generally.

My Analytic Strategy

I'm not sure that all Christian commentators have carefully thought out the best way to evaluate Christians. In using data to judge how Christians are doing, what standards should we use?

Many analyses of Christianity use one of two standards, both of which are problematic. The first standard is perfection. Any deviation of Christianity from the ideal is a cause for alarm. Certainly perfection is our goal, but it's an unattainable goal, and while we can use it for motivation, it's a poor standard for evaluation because no one will ever meet it. Using this standard, we should be alarmed about every single aspect of Christianity. Furthermore, with this standard, we don't need to collect any data about Christians because, by assumption, we've fallen short. I once heard Chuck Colson say that God makes Christians better, not necessarily good. By this he meant that many Christians start off in bad places, and even significant improvement leaves them short sometimes. As such, Christianity can make a substantial difference in peoples' lives, but they can still be far from perfect.

A second commonly used standard is a variation of Supreme Court Justice Potter Stewart's famous comment about pornography—that he can't define it but he knows it when he sees it. Here, commentators do not have any *a priori* standards of evaluation, and instead they use their own judgment in identifying where Christians fall short. The problem here is that we each have our own biases and values with which we evaluate data, and so this approach often tells us more about the person making the evaluations than the group being evaluated.

Rather than using standards of perfection or idiosyncratic judgments, this book makes three other types of comparisons. First, Christians are compared to members of other religions as well as those who have no religious affiliation at all.[10] Breaking it down further, when data allow, I also compare Protestants to Catholics, and among Protestants, Evangelicals to Mainline Protestants and to members of historically Black denominations. This type of comparison allows us to see how Christians are doing compared to other groups, and also to see which Christian groups are doing the best on any given issue.

To illustrate the value of such a comparison, what if I told you that an athlete was successful at doing something 4 out of 10 times, and then I asked you if this meant that she was good? Before answering, you would probably want to know how other players do at it.

If the "something" is hitting a baseball, 4 hits in 10 at bats makes the player among the world's best. If it's shooting free throws, the player is pretty bad. A simple way to evaluate people is to compare them with others.

Also, I compare Christians who attend church frequently to those who attend less frequently. The logic here is that if being a Christian makes a difference in people's lives, we would expect to see more difference among those people who are more involved in it. I use attendance as a measure of involvement since it is commonly collected in many data sets, and it's a relatively straightforward question for respondents to answer.[11]

Finally, when the data are available, I examine Christians' changes over time. On a given measure, are Christians getting better, worse, or staying about the same? Unfortunately, most data sets do not have suitable data for this type of analysis, but I present them when feasible.

Cautions

At this point I would like to issue several cautions in interpreting the analyses of this book. My goal is to simply describe religious differences with no attempt to explain what causes them. Actually developing and testing explanations for these differences becomes enormously complex, and it usually takes us—at least with survey data—to the land of "multivariate analysis," a place where researchers live but few others dare to visit. In fact, trying to explain the findings presented in any one figure in this book would probably require a separate article, if not a whole book in and of itself. Rather, this book simply describes religious differences. But given the many misconceptions about these differences, this is a needed exercise.

On a related point, each religious difference reported in this book is open to multiple causal interpretations.[12] For example, later in this book you'll read that Christians are significantly less likely to smoke marijuana than non-Christians. This could mean that Christianity makes people less likely to smoke marijuana. It could also mean that people who smoke marijuana are less apt to join Christianity. Or maybe Christians who smoke marijuana are more likely to leave their faith. Finally, it could be that some underlying characteristic, say a propensity for conventional behavior, both increases churchgoing while decreasing substance abuse, so there might be no causal relationship between the two at all.

Finally, it's worth noting the limitations of survey data themselves. They allow us to describe social groups along many different dimensions, but by themselves they can be both superficial and incomplete. This is why sociologists routinely complement survey research with other research methods, such as ethnographic studies and experiments. The analogy has been made that analyzing a population with survey data is like flying over a city in a helicopter. There is a lot you can learn from viewing a city from the air, but it is far from a complete picture.[13]

CHAPTER 2

Is American Christianity on the Brink of Extinction?

Evangelical Christianity in America is dying.
—*Christine Wicker, The Fall of the Evangelical Nation*

We are on the verge—within ten years—of a major collapse of evangelical Christianity.
—*Michael Spencer, Internetmonk.com*

The cure for most of our country's problems would be found in a return to the beliefs and morals of America's Founding Fathers.
—*American Heritage Ministry*

A funny thing happened to American religion on the way to the new millennium—some people wanted out. Maybe they kept their religious beliefs, but they stopped affiliating with an organized religion, which, here in the United States, usually means Christianity.

To explore this change, I'll present data from various sources.

Before I do, however, let's briefly review where I'm getting my data. Probably the most useful, and most used, data for the study of American religion is the General Social Survey. It's the Cadillac of national studies because it has been collected every year or two since 1972, and thus it allows us to track changes in religious beliefs, attitudes, and affiliation. Do you want to know if Christians read the Bible more now than they did in past decades? Do you want to know how many Christians are living together before marriage? Do you want to know how many Christians have volunteered to help homeless people? The General Social Survey is your data set. The main limitation of the General Social Survey, however, is that each wave only collects data from several thousand respondents. This is plenty for studying Christianity because so many Americans are Christians, but it's too small to analyze properly other religions with fewer American adherents. To illustrate, the latest wave of the General Social Survey, collected in 2008, interviewed over 1,000 Protestants, almost 500 Catholics, but only 39 Jews, 13 Muslims, 7 Hindus, and 15 Buddhists. This means that if we want to compare across religions, we'll sometimes need to use data from other sources.

Fortunately, in recent years, two very large surveys about religion have been collected—The American Religious Identification Study and the Pew Religious Landscape Survey. These studies survey tens of thousands of Americans, meaning that we can examine smaller religions. Unfortunately, these studies, being so big, are collected less frequently, so they aren't as good for tracking changes.

There are some data available from before the 1970s. Starting in the mid-1930s, the Gallup Poll asked basic questions about religion, questions such as whether people believed in God, were members of churches, and attended churches. Prior to the 1930s, there is some data about religion in the U.S., but not very much.

In addition to these data sets, I'll also use data from various surveys that have unique survey questions or a design feature that addresses a particular issue.

So what does all this mean for discussions of religion? There are a lot of things we'd like to know about religion, but some things we just can't answer because the data aren't there (though baseless speculation is always available). In particular, we can speak about religion in America after 1970 with much more authority than we can before 1970, and we know much less, at least in terms of survey findings, about religion before the 1930s.

Okay, enough preface—let's go to the data.

The Rise of the Unaffiliated

Since the early 1970s, the General Social Survey has asked its respondents a basic question about their religious affiliation: "What is your religious preference? Is it Protestant, Catholic, Jewish, some other religion, or no religion?" Figure 2.1 plots the percentage of respondents who have answered "no religion." As you can see, in the 1970s and 1980s, about 7 or 8% of the American adults surveyed stated that they had no religious affiliation. Then in the 1990s, the number doubled to about 14 or 15%, and it's been above that ever since.

Given the magnitude and significance of this change, let's see if we find it with another data set as well. The American Religious Identification Study was collected in 1990, 2001, and 2008. Each time it collected data from at least 50,000 American adults, and it asked them "What is your religion, if any?" In 1990, 8% of respondents answered "no religion," in 2001, 14% did, and in 2008, 15%. I've plotted these data points on Figure 2.1, and as you can see, they closely match the General Social Survey data. We see almost the exact same trend using two high-quality data sets, so we can be pretty sure that it really happened.

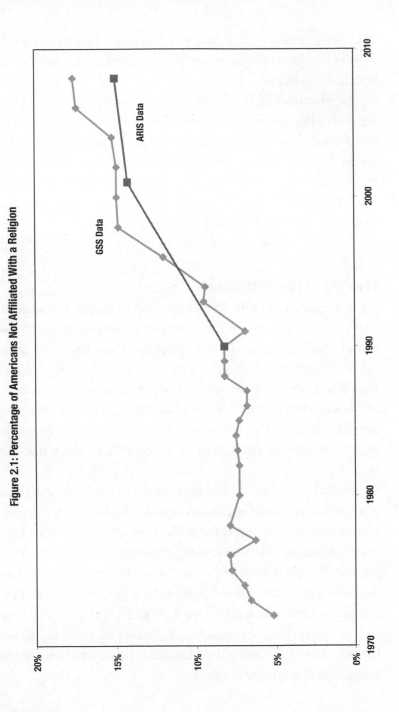

Figure 2.1: Percentage of Americans Not Affiliated With a Religion

Let's call this group of people the "religiously unaffiliated."[1] The obvious question is, what happened in the 1990s to increase their number so dramatically? Perhaps the most persuasive explanation for this change comes from sociologists Michael Hout and Claude Fischer.[2] Analyzing data from the General Social Survey, they found that the increases in religious disaffiliation happened among political liberals and moderates who had relatively weak ties to the church. Disaffiliation did not increase for political conservatives. They concluded that many Christians left the church because of the church's active affiliation with conservative politics.

In the 1980s and 1990s, high-profile evangelical leaders snuggled up with Republican politicians under the banner of the Moral Majority and Christian Coalition. This drove away more liberal members of the Christian church who were at odds with their leaders' conservative agenda. In the current decade, most prominent evangelical leaders in America, such as Rick Warren and Bill Hybels, have not actively supported a given political party, and this might have slowed the rate of religious disaffiliation.

What Hout and Fischer's conclusion warns us is that there may be a substantial cost for the church to play politics—we lose people. Quite possibly, the church would be bigger now without its prior foray into politics. Hout and Fischer write that "had religion not become so politicized, these [unaffiliated] people would have gone on identifying as they had been and the percentage of Americans preferring no religion would have increased only 3 to 4%."[3]

Historian Mark Noll writes that this isn't the first time American Christianity has delved into partisan politics, and doing so had negative consequences the last time as well. Evangelical political activity was especially high in the 1850s, when Evangelicals actively supported the Republican Party in the days leading up to the Civil War. According to one researcher, evangelical ministers were just as enthusiastic about overseeing Republican rallies as revival meetings.

As a result, in the aftermath of the war, evangelical Christianity was factionalized and spiritually spent. Their deep political participation came "at the cost of nearly losing their souls."[4]

While researchers have engaged this increased disaffiliation with curiosity, church leaders and other commentators have responded with near hysteria. Christian apologist Josh McDowell warned that this indeed might be "the last Christian generation" in America.[5] In academic language, but saying pretty much the same thing, R. Albert Mohler Jr, President of the Southern Baptist Seminary, wrote that "the so-called Judeo-Christian consensus of the last millennium has given way to a postmodern, post-Christian, post-Western cultural crisis which threatens the very heart of our culture."[6] *Outreach* magazine writes that "the picture is bleak," the facts are "sobering," and "94% of our churches are losing ground in the communities they serve."[7] Critic Christine Wicker wrote *The Fall of the Evangelical Nation,* in which she claims that "it seems more likely each year that the United States might go the way of Western Europe where Christianity is irrelevant."[8] She summarizes George Barna's work as indicating that "the Evangelical Church as we know it is beginning to die."[9] Quick, put on your chicken costume, because the sky is falling.

A Look at the "Affiliated"

When we look closer at the data, we find a richer, more nuanced story about what's happening with religion in America, and for Evangelicals there is some good news. Let's start with a simple question: Which religions do Americans practice today? The short answer is that we're mostly Christian with some religiously unaffiliated. Figure 2.2 divides Americans' religious affiliations into three groups: Christian, unaffiliated, and all other religions. Three out of 4 Americans affiliate themselves with Christianity; 1 in 6 is religiously unaffiliated; and 1 in 13 practices another religion. As such, the United States is still very much a country of Christians.

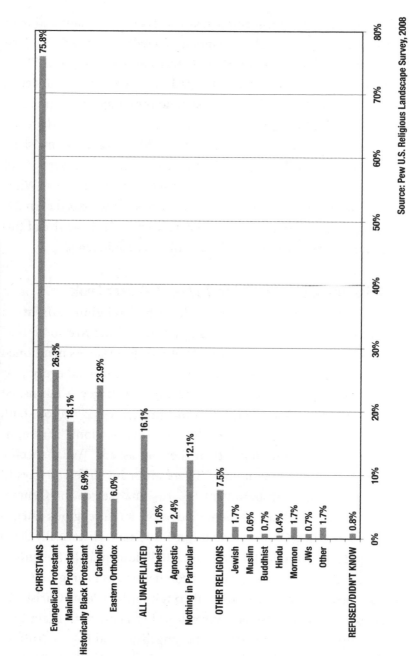

Figure 2.2: Religious Affiliation in America

CHRISTIANS 75.8%
Evangelical Protestant 26.3%
Mainline Protestant 18.1%
Historically Black Protestant 6.9%
Catholic 23.9%
Eastern Orthodox 6.0%
ALL UNAFFILIATED 16.1%
Atheist 1.6%
Agnostic 2.4%
Nothing in Particular 12.1%
OTHER RELIGIONS 7.5%
Jewish 1.7%
Muslim 0.6%
Buddhist 0.7%
Hindu 0.4%
Mormon 1.7%
JWs 0.7%
Other 1.7%
REFUSED/DIDN'T KNOW 0.8%

Source: Pew U.S. Religious Landscape Survey, 2008

Among Christians, about two-thirds are Protestant and one-third Catholic. Among Protestants, about half are Evangelicals. That means that about one-fourth of Americans are evangelical Christians. Among the unaffiliated, only about one-third of them define themselves as agnostic or atheist. The remainder has some mix of spiritual or religious beliefs. Among other religions, there are some that have roots elsewhere in the world, such as Judaism, Islam, Buddhism, and Hinduism. We also have home-grown versions of other religions, such as Mormons and Jehovah's Witnesses.[10] While America has many non-Christian religions, none exceed even 2% of the national population; nonetheless, given the large size of this country, these religions still have millions of adherents.

Religious Affiliation Since 1972—A Closer Look

In the previous section, I described religious affiliation today, but how has it been changing over time? Are some religions increasing in numbers while others decrease? As mentioned earlier, the General Social Survey has been collected every year or two since the early 1970s, and in each survey it has asked respondents: "What is your religious preference? Is it Protestant, Catholic, Jewish, some other religion, or no religion?" If respondents answer "Protestant," then they are asked: "What specific denomination is that, if any?" There are many different ways to categorize these affiliations.[11] For my analyses of the General Social Survey, I'll use a scheme based on seven religious categories: Evangelical Christian, Mainline Protestant, Historically Black Protestant, Catholic, Jewish, Other Religion, and No Religion.[12]

Evangelical Christians have been defined as having four central convictions: (1) salvation through faith in Jesus Christ, (2) an experience of personal conversion (i.e., being born again), (3) the importance of missions and evangelism, and (4) the truth of the Bible.[13] Evangelical denominations include Southern Baptists,

Pentecostals, Charismatics, Assemblies of God, Lutherans in the Missouri Synod, the Church of Christ, and most nondenominational Protestant churches.

Mainline denominations tend to be more moderate or liberal than Evangelicals with regard to their theological orthodoxy and personal lifestyle. Also, they often express a strong sense of ethical responsibility in the public sphere (e.g., social justice) rather than focusing more on individual morality.[14] (In recent years, evangelical churches have followed suit, becoming increasingly involved in issues of social justice.) Mainline denominations include the United Methodist Church, Episcopal Church, Evangelical Lutheran Church in America (ELCA), Presbyterian Church USA, and the United Church of Christ (Congregationalists). These denominations historically came from Europe via immigration in the 1700s and 1800s.

Historically Black denominations share many of the same theological beliefs as Evangelical Christians, but they have a distinct culture that emphasizes the importance of freedom and a quest for justice. While they tend to be more liberal in their economic and political attitudes, they are conservative in social and family issues.[15] Their denominations include the National Baptist Convention, African Methodist Episcopal, and the Church of God in Christ.[16]

Unfortunately, the General Social Survey doesn't collect large enough samples for separate analysis of other, non-Christian religions, such as Judaism, Hinduism, Islam, and Buddhism. Depending on the availability of data, I either clump together all non-Christian religions or I separate out Judaism and then combine the rest.

Figure 2.3 describes Americans' religious affiliation over the past three decades. There are seven different lines on this figure, and each line represents the percentage of General Social Survey respondents in a particular religious group.[17] For example, in 1972, about 30% of all respondents reported being affiliated with a Mainline Protestant church, about 26% of respondents were Catholics, about 20% were

Evangelicals, and so on. As shown in Figure 2.3, there has been both change and stability in American religion since the 1970s. Among Christian groups, Evangelicals grew to about 25% of the population by the 1990s, and have remained there since, perhaps dropping a percentage point or two. Catholics have remained remarkably stable, at about 25 to 26%. Black Protestants have steadily hovered at 8 to 9%. The big story in Christianity, however, is that Mainline Protestantism has decreased dramatically over the past several decades. They have fallen from over 30% of the population to less than 15%—a tremendous change that has happened steadily over time and has shown no sign of abating.

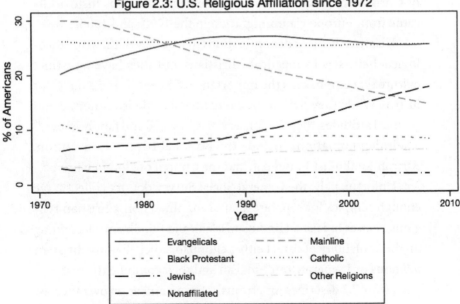

Figure 2.3: U.S. Religious Affiliation since 1972

Source : General Social Survey

Among other religious groups, Jews have stayed steady at 2 to 3% of the population, and members of other religions have increased from about 3 to 6%. The other big change, in addition to the drop in Mainline Protestants, has been the increase in the religiously unaffiliated, as discussed at the start of this chapter.

To understand these changes better, let's take a look at the religious groups separately. Starting with Evangelicals, while their representation in the country has stayed fairly stable in recent decades, the form of their affiliation has changed. In particular, an increasing number of Evangelical Christians now describe themselves in general terms such as *nondenominational, born again,* or just *Christian* instead of using denominational labels such as Baptist or Evangelical Free. Reflecting this change, in 1990, only about 200,000 Americans described themselves as nondenominational Christians, but in 2008, 8 million did so.[18]

The continued strength of evangelical Christianity in the United States poses a puzzle. Why have Evangelicals thrived in such a diverse society that many Evangelicals believe actively opposes Christianity? Sociologist Christian Smith offers a compelling answer. He posits that American evangelical Christianity has prospered *because* its members perceive society as opposed to them and as threatening their faith. This distinction between the church and secular society has various benefits. It provides identity and meaning for Evangelical Christians. It defines them as group members and increases their commitment to their group. Also, the existence of other religious options reinforces our understanding of evangelical belief as a choice rather than merely an expectation of society, and this too increases commitment. Ironically, the contemporary forces of secularism, pluralism, and postmodernism that Evangelicals sometimes denounce might actually help keep the church strong.[19]

Another reason given by sociologists for the size of evangelical Christianity, at least relative to mainline churches, regards a factor that many Christians haven't thought of—differential fertility rates. Children born into a given religion are more likely to remain in that religion as adults. For example, more adult Catholics were born into Catholic families than into Protestant or Muslim families. We'll look at this dynamic more in the next chapter, but for now let's just assume that it's generally true. This being the case, religions or religious groups whose members have the most children should, all else being equal, grow the fastest. This helps explain the growth rates of Evangelicals and Mainline Protestants, for Conservative Protestant Christian women have historically had more children than Mainline Protestant women. In the early 1900s, conservative Christians averaged one more child per family than more liberal Christians, and current projections place the difference at .3 children more.[20] Certainly there is more to religious change than fertility rates, but it does seem to be a piece of the puzzle.

The decline of Mainline Protestantism has been dramatic, probably representing the biggest change in the American religious landscape in the past century. Just thirty years ago, Mainline Protestants were the largest religious group in the United States, and now they are the fourth, behind Evangelicals, Catholics, and the religiously unaffiliated. What happened? We've already covered two explanations—a reaction to Christianity being seen as politically conservative and differential fertility rates. In addition, there are two other popular explanations.

One explanation holds that Mainline Protestantism has decreased because it is not strict enough and is, ironically, too accommodating. Strict religions demand more time, money, and commitment from their members, and this fact results in members finding more meaning in their faith. Perhaps counterintuitively, religions that make it easy for their members also provide fewer benefits and garner less commitment. Mainline Protestants, being relatively lenient in what they ask of their members, have consequently lost members.[21]

Another explanation comes from church growth literature. Every year the American population grows. This means that if a religious group wants to keep pace, they need to provide increasingly more opportunities for people to attend their services. It's estimated that for a Christian denomination not to lose ground, it must yearly plant one new church for every 100 existing churches. Whereas evangelical groups have emphasized church planting, most mainline churches have not, and so there are not increased opportunities for people to attend them. In short, the number of Americans has grown every year but the number of seats in mainline churches has not.[22]

Turning to Historically Black denominations, one explanation for their continuance points to the unique functions they provide for their members. Among these functions, Black churches provide leadership opportunities for their members that may not be available outside of the church. Some of the best known African-American politicians and leaders have been closely affiliated with a Christian church, people such as Martin Luther King Jr., Jesse Jackson, and Al Sharpton. Black churches also provide important social services such as food, clothing, and housing for their members in need.[23]

The percentage of Catholic Americans has remained quite steady over the years. This could be interpreted as the Catholic Church having a stable membership, but in fact these numbers disguise a considerable amount of change among Catholics. Notably, a large number of American-born Catholics have left their religion; in fact, an estimated 10% of all Americans are former Catholics.[24] Why, then, hasn't the percentage of Catholics plummeted? Immigration. A disproportionate number of immigrants to the United States are Catholic, most from Hispanic countries. Whereas about 21% of native-born Americans are Catholic, 46% of immigrants are Catholic.[25] As a result, almost one-quarter of American Catholics are foreign-born, compared to only 6% of Protestants.[26] The substantial immigration of Catholics has balanced the continued loss of domestically born Catholics, producing steady overall numbers of Catholics in the country.

Regarding other religions, membership in non-Christian

41

religions has more than doubled since the early 1970s, going from about 4% of the national population to 8%. Despite this growth, the overall share of other religions is relatively small. As shown earlier, in Figure 2.1, Mormons and Jews constitute less than 2% of the nation's population, and Buddhists, Hindus, and Muslims less than 1%.

Many people overestimate the size of these other religions. One study concluded that "both the size of these [non-Christian] groups and their growth has often been exaggerated."[27] This misperception is evidenced in a 2008 *Newsweek* poll.[28] It asked the question: "The vast majority of Americans are Christians. Which of the following is the largest group of non-Christians in the United States: Jews, Muslims, Buddhists, or the unaffiliated?" The correct answer, of course, is "unaffiliated" by almost a 10 to 1 margin, but barely a third of the respondents got it correct. Here are the results:

- 25% of the respondents said Jews
- 20% said Muslims
- 4% said Buddhists
- 38% said the unaffiliated
- 13% said they didn't know

The growth of other religions has varied by religion. Islam and Hinduism have grown largely due to immigration, since two-thirds of Muslims in America are immigrants, as are a full 80% of Hindus. In contrast, most Buddhists are U.S.-born, either being born into a Buddhist family or having converted as an adult.[29]

A Closer Look at the Unaffiliated

Finally, let's examine the religiously unaffiliated, for there is a lot of misconception about them. Both media presentations and popular discussions of this group routinely, and erroneously, identify them as all atheists, agnostics, secular humanists, or other unbelievers. This is certainly true of some of the unaffiliated, but many of them believe in God yet choose not to affiliate with a given religion.

As an example of this confusion, in 2009, *The New York Times* published an article about atheists in the United States.[30] They printed a map that pulled data from the American Religious Identification Survey on the number of religiously unaffiliated. The caption on the map, however, equated having no religious affiliation with being an atheist. The map was titled "Fewer Christians, More Atheists in 2008," and below this title was written, "Since 1990, the percentage of Americans identifying themselves as Christians has decreased to 77% from 86%. Atheists, however, have gained ground in every state; 15% of Americans now identify themselves as nonbelievers."

So who are the religiously unaffiliated? It turns out that many of them are religious. As shown in Figure 2.4, it is true that they rarely attend religious services—only 8% of them attend even monthly. However, the majority (56%) of them believe in God. Another 22% believe in a higher power. Only 8% of the religiously unaffiliated actually do not believe in God (i.e., are atheists), and another 14% believe there is no way to know for sure if there is a God (i.e., agnosticism). Over half (55%) believe that the Bible is either the literal or inspired Word of God, whereas 41% view it as a book of fables. Forty-nine percent pray daily or weekly and only 25% never pray. About half view themselves as religious to some degree, and three-fourths view themselves as spiritual.[31]

It could be that the increase in the number of religiously unaffiliated does not reflect a change in Americans' beliefs and values as much as it does a new willingness and openness to not identify with a religion. In the past there may have been enough stigma associated with being unaffiliated that some people would affiliate with a religion more out of custom or expectation.[32] As our society has become more accepting of the irreligious, perhaps more

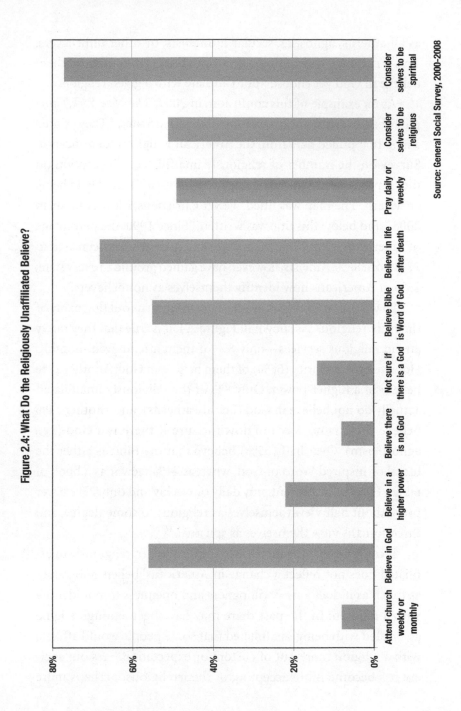

Figure 2.4: What Do the Religiously Unaffiliated Believe?

Source: General Social Survey, 2000–2008

people are willing to step out on their own, not identifying with an organized religion even if they remain religious at a personal level. Our society is more accepting of those who don't affiliate, whether they are at some level "believers" or not. As stated in the American Religious Identification Survey report (page 7), "The historic reluctance of Americans to self-identify as [atheists and agnostics] or use these terms seems to have diminished."

As a way of examining this issue, I have plotted levels of belief in God, as recorded in the General Social Survey. This question asks respondents: "Which statement comes closest to expressing what you believe about God?" and the possible statements reflect atheism, agnosticism, believing in a higher power, or believing in God with varying levels of certainty or doubt. Unfortunately, this question has been collected only five times by the GSS, starting in 1988, but that should be enough to observe trends. As shown in Figure 2.5, theological beliefs about God have remained fairly steady over the past twenty years. There is some decline in believing in God, and a corresponding increase in the other three forms of belief, but the magnitude of these changes is much less than the increased number of religiously unaffiliated. This observation reinforces the idea that this increase often reflects a change in status in regard to the church, not so much in terms of personal religious beliefs.

The discussion of religious groups so far has examined them in terms of their percentage of the population. This makes sense because each year the population of the United States grows, and using percentages allows us to compare current and previous levels of affiliation. Nonetheless, this focus on percentages can obscure the point that a religious group can grow in absolute numbers while remaining stable or even declining in terms of percentages.

In terms of the number of American adults in various religious groups, several groups have had considerable growth in recent decades.[33] Since 1972, Evangelical Christians have more than doubled in number, going from about 25 million adults to almost 60 million. Likewise, the number of Catholics, religiously unaffiliated, and members of other religions grew considerably. The number of Black Protestants and Jews remained mostly stable, and the number of Mainline Protestants dropped, from over 40 million to less than 35 million.

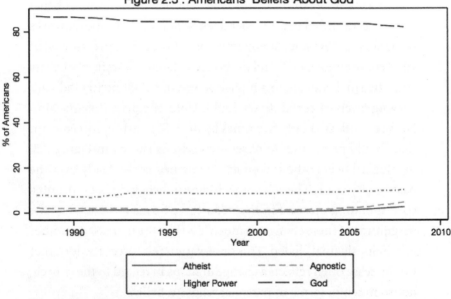

Figure 2.5 : Americans' Beliefs About God

Source : General Social Survey

Religious Affiliation Since 1910—General Social Survey

The data presented so far starts in the early 1970s. These are the most accurate data available, and they allow us to track changes over the last several decades, but wouldn't it be interesting to know about Americans' religious behavior before that? Well, tucked away in the General Social Survey is an intriguing question: "In what religion were you raised?" On one hand, this question is probably less accurate than asking people about their current religious affiliation, for it requires people to remember back to their youth. On the other hand, it's not unreasonable to assume that most people can accurately answer it, given the significance of one's religious upbringing. For example, I can answer the question with certainty. (I was raised in the Catholic Church, by the way). This question gives us data stretching back to the early 1900s since some of the respondents were already in their sixties and seventies when they were interviewed in the 1970s.[34]

What are the long-term trends? Evangelical Christianity has held steady at around 25% of the population. Mainline Christianity has declined steadily since the early 1900s—not just in the last forty years. Black Protestants grew through the first half of the century, and then stabilized at about 10% thereafter. Catholics grew through the 1970s, after which they have leveled off. Other religions have fluctuated around 6% of the population with a slow, continuous increase over time. The religiously unaffiliated were rare before the 1970s, after which they have increased each decade.

Religious Beliefs and Practices Since 1935—Gallup Data

Another way of looking at religion in America, in addition to religious affiliation, is to look at the religious beliefs of Americans as a whole. The well-known Gallup organization conducted some of the very first national surveys, and George Gallup himself had an interest in religion; therefore, they provide data about religion in the United States for the last seventy years or so.[35] These data do not provide the in-depth, detailed information that we might like, but they do describe long-term trends of religion during the twentieth century. Three of the questions that Gallup asks most often include: "Are you a member of a church?" "Did you attend church last week?" and "Do you believe in God?"[36]

Figure 2.6 presents the Gallup data. The first question is with regard to belief in God, and while it has decreased a bit over the decades, the percentage of Americans who believe in God has remained remarkably high—over 90% of Americans have believed and continue to believe in some form of God. In reference to this continued high level of belief in God, one researcher commented that "this stability [of belief in God] is all the more remarkable in light of the dramatic social, economic, and political changes over the past half-century."[37]

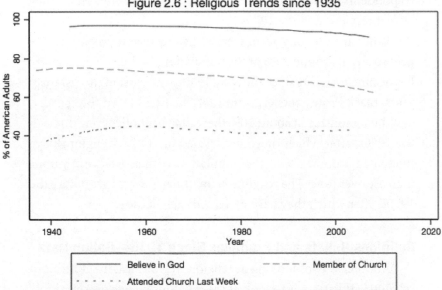

Figure 2.6 : Religious Trends since 1935

Source : Gallup Surveys

As we'll see in a later chapter, people's understanding of the nature of God and how certain they are that God exists has changed over the decades, but the stability of belief in God is, well, remarkable. The second question asks if Americans are members of a church, and it has shown more change. In the 1940s, about 75% of Americans reported being church members, and now the number is down to almost 60%. The third question asks about church attendance. Reported attendance rates increased in the 1940s and 1950s, and they have been mostly stable since then, with a little over 40% of Americans reporting that they attended church in the prior week. As I'll discuss in a later chapter, there is controversy among sociologists as to whether people overstate how often they go to church on survey questions. As such, the actual last-week attendance rates might be somewhat lower than shown in Figure 2.6. However, assuming that any over-reporting has been about the same each decade, then the attendance data presented here is accurate regarding year-to-year change or stability.

Religious Adherence Since 1776—Census and Church Membership Rolls

Let's go back even further in American history to the founding of our country. It's my impression that many Christians today perceive the colonial era as a golden age of Christianity—when great men such as George Washington and Thomas Jefferson founded a Christian country and the common folk followed God with reverence and humility. In fact, a recent survey found that three-fourths of conservative Christians believe that the United States was founded as a Christian nation.[38] Politically conservative Christians routinely hold up our Founding Fathers as the religious model for today. Reflecting this, several Christian ministries have been established to advance the significance of early-American Christianity for today's world.[39] One of them, Reclaiming America for Christ, has expressed this viewpoint in its mission statement:

> Our Mission is to educate our pastors, legislators, educators, students and all citizens as to the truth about America's Christian Heritage and the role of fundamental, biblical Christianity in the establishment and function of our legal, legislative and educational systems; and to work towards the successful reestablishment of these values in our society today.[40]

If we were to plot the history of American Christianity as it is sometimes talked about in Christian circles, we might identify three supposed phases: from the Revolution through perhaps the 1950s, we were a strong, Christian country; then in the 1960s, the country started its slide down into secular godlessness; and at the present moment we're facing a crisis. Christianity might plummet to extinction in the near future. Figure 2.7 illustrates what this scenario might look like if we put it into a graph.

Figure 2.7: Hypothetical Religious Adherence Rates in U.S. History

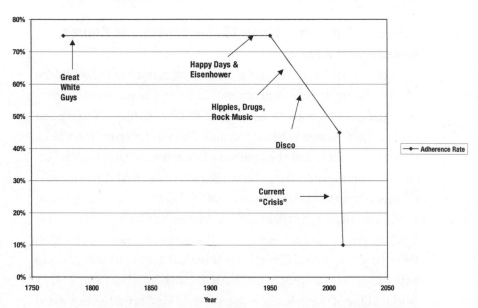

What has really happened in American history? In a perfect world, we would have Ye Olde General Survey dating back 200 years to give us precise data on Americans' beliefs and affiliations throughout history. While we don't have nationally representative surveys from back then, that doesn't mean we have no data. At the time of the Revolution, various denominations kept detailed statistics about their membership. From 1850 to 1936, the United States Census Bureau collected statistical data about church bodies. They stopped, by the way, after World War II when members of the Jewish community expressed understandable fears that enumerating the Jewish presence in the United States might further inflame anti-Semitism.[41] Since World War II, various agencies and organizations have stepped in and collected data.

Two sociologists, Roger Finke and Rodney Stark, gathered these historical data, and they used them to calculate Americans' religious adherence at ten points in time—1776, 1850, 1860, 1870, 1890, 1906, 1916, 1926, 1952, and 1980. Figure 2.8 presents their calculations in terms of adherence rates—how many Americans adhered to religion in each of these years. (In this context, religious adherence means about the same thing as church membership.)[42] As shown, actually very few Americans were church members during the Revolutionary era—less than 1 in 5. The big change happened with the Second Great Awakening, in the early 1800s, the time of Charles Finney and revival meetings. During this time, adherence rates jumped to about one-third. In the late 1800s, they jumped again, to almost half of the population, and they have steadily risen to the present when almost two-thirds of the nation adheres to a religion.

I imagine that the data presented in Figure 2.8 would surprise most Americans today because we commonly assume early America to be the golden era of religious faith. How can we be so wrong about our religious history? Nostalgia is remarkably powerful, and thinking that we used to be great—along whatever dimensions— makes us feel good about ourselves and our country. Finke and Stark put it this way:

> America is burdened with more nostalgic illusions about the colonial era than any other period in their history. Our concep- tions of that time are dominated by a few powerful illustrations of Pilgrim scenes that most people over forty stared at year after year on classroom walls: the baptism of Pocahontas, the Pilgrims walking through the woods to church, the first Thanksgiving. Had these classroom walls also been graced with colonial scenes of drunken revelry and ballroom brawling, of women in risqué ball-gowns, of gamblers and rakes, a better balance might have been struck.[43]

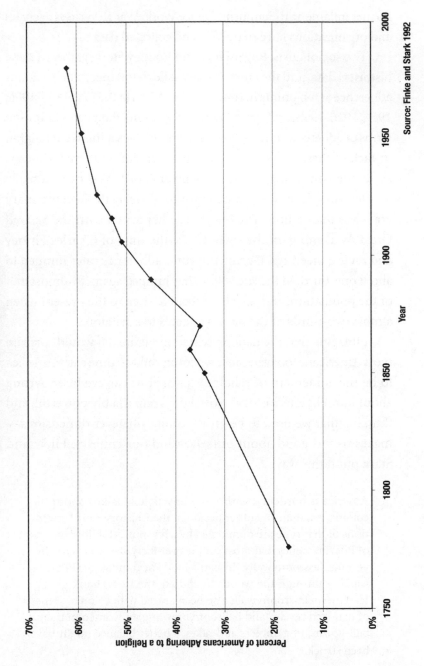

Figure 2.8: Rates of Religious Adherence, 1776-1980

Source: Finke and Stark 1992

Various factors underlay the apparent irreligion in colonial America.[44] Many of the Europeans who emigrated here had weak family attachments, were on the run from punishment, or left their homes in shame—not necessarily the kind of people who usually have deep religious convictions. In fact, the English courts sent up to 50,000 criminals to the Colonies. Also, at the time, much of the United States was a frontier, and a frontier-ethos often does not emphasize religion. Frontiers also attract more men than women, and men tend to be less religious than women, at least when it comes to Christianity.

Ironically, many of the Founding Fathers revered by today's Christians would not be defined or accepted as Christians if they were alive today.[45] While George Washington and John Adams had Christian convictions, Thomas Jefferson, if he were taking a survey, would have probably checked the box "higher power." Ben Franklin? He went from atheist to polytheist.[46] Historian Mark Noll writes that evangelical Christianity, as we understand it today, only became important in the United States after 1800. The religious faith during the colonial era, though Protestant, was not what we currently refer to as evangelical. Many of the Founding Fathers were either deists or simply supporters of their European-based denominations, which did not stress the need for conversion or personal piety as do modern Evangelicals.[47]

Is God Dead?

Religion's continued prominence in America counters the predictions of many high-profile social thinkers. In 1882, German philosopher Friedrich Nietzsche declared, "God is dead."[48] He didn't mean that God had suffered a physical death, like slipping on an icy planet or something, but rather that humans had lost their ability to believe in God; therefore religions, like Christianity, had lost their moral basis and would not last long. Nietzsche wasn't the first or the last person to predict the decline of organized religion. Here are a few other predictions by famous people:

- In 1710, English thinker Thomas Woolston said Christianity would be gone by 1900.
- Voltaire said religion would crumble within fifty years.
- Famous dead-white-guys Karl Marx, Friedrich Engels, and Sigmund Freud each predicted that religion soon would disappear.
- Renowned sociologist Peter Berger wrote in 1968 that in "the 21st century, religious believers are likely to be found only in small sects, huddled together to resist a worldwide secular culture."

Sociologists have referred to this general idea as "secularization"—that societies irreversibly transition from sacred to secular principles. Certainly there have been meaningful changes in both the form and nature of religion in America, but these changes have not fit the expectation that American Christianity would die. Peter Berger has recognized the error of his prediction, and he has written since:

> The assumption that we live in a secularized world is false. The world today, with some exceptions . . . is as furiously religious as it ever was, and in some places more so than ever. This means that a whole body of literature by historians and social scientists loosely labeled "secularization theory" is essentially mistaken.[49]

To paraphrase Mark Twain: "The reports of God's death are greatly exaggerated."

Are Recent Changes Bad?

The continued vitality of religion in the United States does not obscure the fact that the number of religiously unaffiliated Americans has increased substantially in recent years. This raises an interesting question—is this disaffiliation a bad thing for the church? Many would answer yes, viewing it as the beginning of the end of Christianity. For example, *Newsweek* magazine, in writing about the religiously unaffiliated, put on its cover: "The End of Christian America."

Another approach, however, comes from Mark Driscoll—a controversial pastor in the Seattle area.[50] Driscoll distinguishes active, practicing Christians from those who simply profess Christianity without any deeper engagement. Presumably, it is the second category of "cultural" Christians who are redefining themselves as unaffiliated. If so, Driscoll argues, then there is little drop-off in active, committed Christians, and the church doesn't suffer much from the loss of less-committed members. As a result, the remaining Christians are more likely to live in accord with Christian principles and thus better represent the church.[51] Driscoll concludes that recent changes "are not discouraging, but rather clarifying." Driscoll's argument makes a larger point: Numerical declines are not necessarily negative.[52] We need to critically evaluate what is happening and think through its implications for the church.

CHAPTER 3

Are We Losing Our Young People? What Will Happen in the Future?

It is clear that we have all but lost our young people to a godless culture.

—*Josh McDowell, Christian apologist*

Eighty-eight percent of evangelical children are leaving the church shortly after they graduate from high school.

—*Southern Baptist Convention Council on Family Life*

Christianity will go. It will vanish and shrink.

—*John Lennon*

Now for a subject that causes great fear and anxiety for Christians: What is happening to our young people? This subject, probably more than any other covered in this book, generates overheated hyperbole. Listen to what church leaders and commentators have said. A well-known apologist for the Christian faith claims that "between sixty-nine and ninety-four percent of their young people are leaving the traditional church after high school . . . and very few are returning."[1] Wanting to make sure that we all understand the significance of these statistics, he writes to the reader: "I sincerely believe that unless something is done now to change the spiritual state of our young people—you will become the last Christian generation!"[2]

An article in a Christian magazine asks, "Are We Losing Our Young People?" and it claims that only 1 in 4 members of youth groups will stay in the Christian community after they graduate.[3] Other commentators warn that a great majority of Christian youth will "disengage," "stop attending," "leave the foundations of their faith," and "forsake their faith."[4]

Let me give an extended example, told by sociologist Christian Smith, of how badly Christians can mangle statistics when it comes to discussions of our youth.[5] A four-page advertisement in evangelical Christianity's flagship magazine boldly states: "Christianity in America won't survive another decade unless we do something now." Why? "This generation of teens is the largest in history—and current trends show that only 4% will be evangelical believers by the time they become adults. . . . We are on the verge of a catastrophe."

Where did this 4% figure come from? Ten years ago a seminary professor did an informal survey of 211 young people interviewed in three states. The question was poorly worded, and the study probably used a convenience sample. In terms of quality, this statistic is about as valid as someone putting a survey question on their Facebook page and then having their friends and acquaintances answer it. There's nothing wrong with doing it, it's just not very trustworthy. Motivated by this questionable statistic, a Christian organization was asking tens of thousands of youth pastors around the country to spend $39 to attend a conference on how to avoid this coming catastrophe. The advertisement featuring the statistic had pictures of some of the best-known evangelical leaders in the country, implying that they endorsed the message of this conference.[6]

This raises an interesting question: Why would the organization sponsoring the conference highlight such a problematic statistic when there are plenty of reliable statistics about Christian youth available? I don't presume to know the motivations of the conference organizers, but it's entirely possible that they chose the "4% statistic" for its shock value—as a way of drawing people to their conference—rather than for its accuracy.

Just for a moment, let's stop and think about what it would look like if these dire warnings were to come true. There are around 80 million kids under the age of eighteen in America. About two-thirds of them have been raised in a Christian tradition. This means that for current adults to be the last Christian generation, somewhere around 50 million young people have to leave the faith. How would this happen? Will millions of them just decide that "I was going to believe in God, but I sure like that cool new video game that just came out"? Or will they think, "I just met a non-Christian, and I think I'll be one too"? Trying to envision this massive, abrupt social change points to its absurdity.

Without even looking at data, we can find problems with these dire predictions. They assume that something has gone wrong with today's youth, but in contrast, previous generations of young people got things right, so that they, unlike today's kids, were able to adhere to their faith through the turmoil of growing up. Here's what I want to know: Who were these young spiritual giants of yesteryear? I was actually a young person myself once, graduating from high school in 1980, and I sure didn't see many spiritual giants hanging around. In fact, let me offer you proof-positive of the brokenness and depravity of my generation—a picture of me and my best friend Hobby. There I am on the right, with a scowl, longish hair, and a disco-print shirt. Now look closely at the picture—do you think the adults of that generation had any faith in the future based on teens like us? No way. And, it wasn't just my generation. The generation after me survived the Yuppie era—a time of rampant greed and selfishness. The generation before mine was a bunch of hippies—I think they were all stoned. Now, if ever there was a generation of young people that would undo Christianity, it was young people in the 1960s—they rejected everything conventional. Now, however, they are writing books and giving sermons about the problems of today's youth.

The problem with these predictions is that every generation frets about the morals of their youth—it's what adults do. For example:

- In 1976, a divinity professor published a book expressing the same worries about the youth then. Its title: *Will Our Children Have Faith?*

- In the 1920s, sociologists conducted an in-depth community study of Muncie, Indiana. They found that parents routinely complained about how their teenagers have too much freedom and get into trouble.

- In 2800 BC, an Assyrian stone tablet lamented that "our earth is degenerate in these latter days . . . children no longer obey their parents."

As long as I'm on the topic of predictions, let me make my own. In 100 years, our great-great-grandchildren will be worried about the morals and religious behavior of our great-great-great-grandchildren.

It's actually rather complex to interpret data about young people. If older people are different than young people, it could reflect generational differences rather than age differences. Maybe people born in a particular generation will always be different than those born in other generations. For example, we talk about Baby-Boomers versus Generation X-ers. What factors shaped these generations? Perhaps older people lived through a given event that younger people did not, and this event changed them. Those who lived through the Great Depression or World War II may always have a different outlook than those who did not.

On the other hand, differences between the young and the old could be due to their ages. For example, older people tend to have more gray hair than the young, but some day the young will get old and gray themselves. Likewise, it's common for generations to get more politically conservative as they age.

What does all this mean for studying young people in the church? Well, if young people have different religious attitudes and behaviors than older people, it can be difficult to know exactly why these differences exist. Maybe each generation is becoming progressively less religious, and so eventually religion will die out. But perhaps young people are less religious in every generation, and they grow up to be more religious as they get older. Viewed this way, religious changes are part of the normal life cycle of aging. Or maybe, as a third option, some event has made a particular generation less religious than previous generations, but future generations will return to the previously high levels.[7]

With this caution in mind, let's look at data to find out what's really happening to our young people. Let's start by comparing people of different ages. If, in fact, we're losing the young, then we would expect to see a much greater increase in religious non-affiliation among them than other age groups. Figure 3.1 plots the percentage of Americans who were religiously unaffiliated in recent decades, breaking the numbers down by age. Sure enough, we see an increase in non-affiliation among young people. Only about 12% of young adults (ages 18–29) in the 1970s and 1980s did not affiliate with a religion. Since the 1990s, that number has doubled to 25%. However, we also see the same pattern with the other age groups. In fact, the percentage of the religiously unaffiliated just about tripled among people in their thirties, forties, fifties, and sixties. For example, only 3.4% of people in their fifties were unaffiliated in the 1970s, but now it's about 14%. The increase in religious non-affiliation is happening in all age groups—not just among the young. Maybe we should be writing articles about how we're "losing" the middle-aged.

We can also look at young people's religious affiliation over time. Are fewer and fewer of them affiliating with Christianity? Figure 3.2 plots the religious affiliation of 18 to 29-year-olds in the last four decades. As shown, religious affiliation trends among young people are similar to those of the general adult population, as described in the previous chapter. Since the 1970s, between 20 and 25% of young people have been affiliated with evangelical Christianity. Currently, 22% of young adults affiliate with evangelical churches, down from 25% in the 1990s, but up from 21% in the 1970s. There has been a substantial drop of young Mainline Protestants, and Catholics have remained steady, perhaps showing a slight drop. The number of youth in Black Protestant churches and other religions has remained mostly stable. Religious non-affiliation has increased substantially.

Let's ask a more general question: Are American young people becoming less religious over time? We can address this question using data from the Monitoring the Future Study. This study interviews about 15,000 high school seniors a year, and it has done so

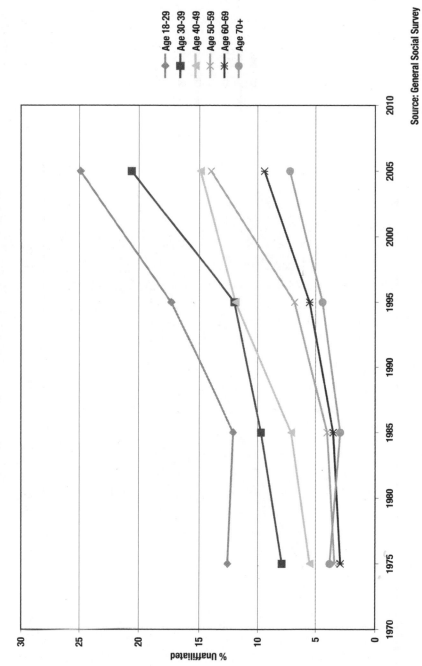

Figure 3.1: Percentage of Religious Unaffiliation Over Time by Age

Source: General Social Survey

Age 18-29
Age 30-39
Age 40-49
Age 50-59
Age 60-69
Age 70+

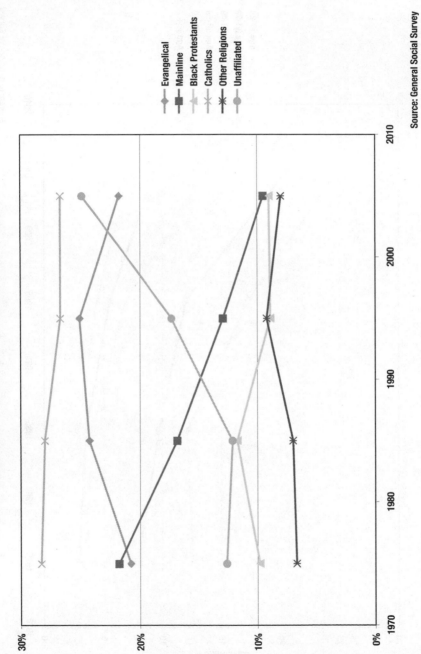

Figure 3.2: Percentage of Religious Affiliation of Young Adults (18-29) by Decade

Source: General Social Survey

since 1975. It asks them about a variety of topics, including three about their religious values and practices: "What is your religious preference?" "How important is religion in your life?" and "How often do you attend religious services?" The percentage of seniors who reported having any religious affiliation reached a high point in the 1980s, when it was about 90%, and it has since dropped to just above 80%. The percentage of seniors who viewed religion as either "pretty important" or "very important" dropped in the early 1980s, but it remained mostly stable for the next twenty years at between 55 and 60%. Likewise, the number of seniors who attended church on a weekly or monthly basis dropped through the 1980s, but it has held steady since then at about 45 to 50%.

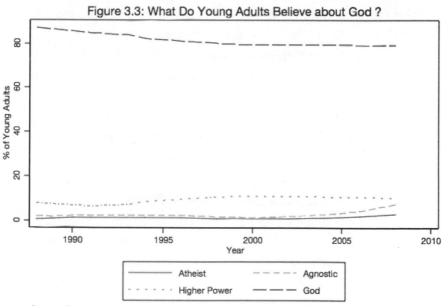

Figure 3.3: What Do Young Adults Believe about God ?

Source : General Social Survey

We can also look at measures of religious beliefs. The General Social Survey asks respondents about their beliefs about God, and the responses can be organized into four separate categories:

(1) believing in a God (albeit with varying levels of certainty), (2) believing in a higher power, (3) not believing in a God (i.e., atheists), and (4) not knowing whether there is a God (i.e., agnostics). Figure 3.3 presents young people's answers to this question since the late 1980s, and, as shown, currently about 8 in 10 young adults believe in God. This number dropped through the early 1990s, but it has remained rather stable since. About 10% or less of young people believe in a higher power or are agnostic, and less than 5% are atheists.

So back to our original question: Is the church really losing the young? On the negative side, the number of young people who do not affiliate with any religion has increased in recent decades, just as it has for the whole population. Furthermore, to the extent that religiousness has changed, it has trended slightly toward less religion. On the positive side, the percentage of young people who attend church or who think that religion is important has remained mostly stable. Also, the percentage that affiliate with Catholicism, evangelical Christianity, and Black protestantism are at or near 1970 levels. What I don't see in the data are evidence of a cataclysmic loss of young people. Have we lost the young? No. Sure, terrible things could happen in the future, but so could great things.

The Relationship Between Age and Religion

Beyond asking if we are losing the young, we can explore more generally the relationship between age and religion. In doing this, we can start with the observation that different religious groups have different age distributions—some have overall older members, others have younger. This age difference is seen in Figure 3.4, which uses data from the 2008 Pew U.S. Religious Landscape Survey. Because this study is so large, with 35,000 respondents, it allows us to compare many of the smaller religious groups in the United States. Using these data, we can see how many members of

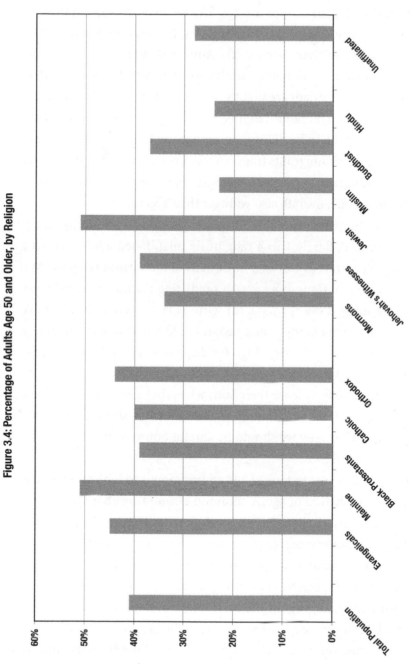

Figure 3.4: Percentage of Adults Age 50 and Older, by Religion

Source: Pew U.S. Religious Landscape Survey, 2008

various religious groups are age fifty or older. As shown, there is some variation across religious groups. In the general population, 41% of all adults are over age fifty. Among Mainline Protestants and Jews, however, over half of adults are over fifty. Evangelicals and Orthodox Christians are slightly older than the population average, Catholics, and Black Protestants. The youngest religious groups are Muslims and Hindus. This is because many U.S. members of these religions are immigrants from other countries, and generally speaking, immigrants tend to be younger than their host population.[8] Mormons are, overall, also younger than average.

Among the youngest religious groups are the religiously unaffiliated. Barely 1 in 4 religiously unaffiliated adults are over fifty in contrast to 1 in 3 (if not 1 in 2) of the various religions. We should be cautious, however, in predicting the future of religions using solely these age data, for various factors come into play. A religion having many young people could reflect that it is growing rapidly, perhaps through high fertility rates. It could also indicate high rates of immigration, or it could mean that its young people are more likely to leave their faith when they get older. We'll look at religious transitions and predictions for the future later in this book, but for now we should be careful not to over-interpret the data in this figure.

Another way to look at age and religion is to look at religiousness as a function of age. A common assumption about religion is that it appeals to the elderly more than the young, and by and large, this assumption is correct. Focusing on Evangelicals, Figure 3.5 plots the percentage of Americans at different ages who are Evangelicals. About 20% of American twenty-year-olds affiliate with evangelical Christianity, and this affiliation rate increases until about age sixty, at which point about 27% are Evangelicals. It decreases slightly in the mid-seventies. Generally speaking, though, older Americans are more likely than younger ones to affiliate with evangelical Christianity.

Why are older people more religious? Previous research has found that young people commonly leave organized religion as they separate from their families, but then they rejoin when they start families of their own.[9] If this is the case, then the young people of any generation are less religious, but this changes as they age. Religion becomes part of the life cycle, along with having kids, buying a house, and whatever else we do as we get older.

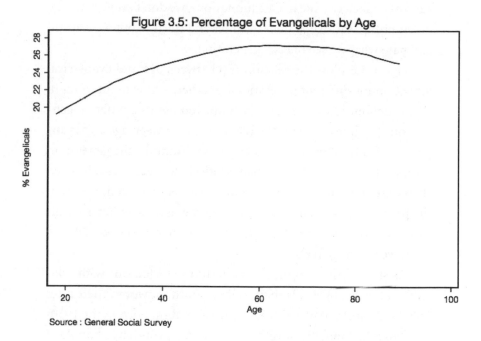

Figure 3.5: Percentage of Evangelicals by Age

Source : General Social Survey

Here is where things get tricky. How do we know that today's young people will become more religious as they age? Well, since we don't have a crystal ball, we can't know for sure what will happen. We can, however, look at what's happened to young people in previous generations. For example, what were today's forty-year-olds like when they were in their twenties? Were they more religious than today's youth? Did they get more religious with age? Figure 3.6 presents this type of analysis. It divides respondents from the General Social Survey into four categories—those born from 1910–1929, 1930–1949, 1950–1969, and 1970–1989. We can think of each one of these four groups as representing a different generation, and we can track each generation over time.[10]

Obviously we don't have full information on each group. For example, respondents in the 1970–1989 group are now younger than forty years old, so we don't know what they will be like after age forty. Likewise, due to data limitations, we don't know what the oldest group was like in their twenties and thirties, but we can still compare what we see of each generation.

Figure 3.6 plots the relationship between age and evangelical affiliation for different generations, and here's how to interpret it. There are four lines on it, and each line represents a different generation. The lines describe the relationship between age and evangelical affiliation for that generation. For example, the generation born in the 1930s and 1940s had relatively few Evangelicals when they were in their twenties—about 19%. As they aged, however, the percentage of them who described themselves as Evangelicals increased so that by the time they were in their seventies, 30% of them were Evangelicals.

As shown, the two oldest generations started out with relatively fewer Evangelicals than today's youth; however, their rates increased substantially with age. The generation born in the 1950s and 1960s had more Evangelicals than today's youth by a couple of percentage points. Therefore, today's youth are starting out with more Evangelicals than their grandparents and great-grandparents, but slightly fewer than their parents. In all four generations, however, evangelical involvement has increased with age.

Based on these data, we might expect that this current generation of young people will follow a similar trend as previous generations;

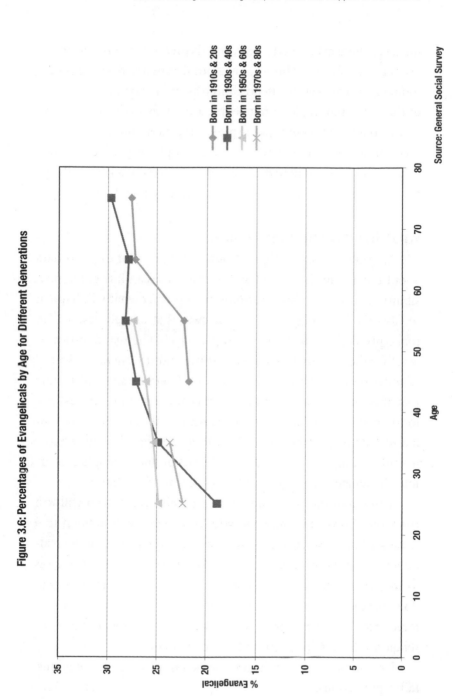

Figure 3.6: Percentages of Evangelicals by Age for Different Generations

Source: General Social Survey

however, there may be some dark clouds on the horizon. Acclaimed sociologist Robert Wuthnow points out that married young people today are just as likely to attend church as the married young people of the 1970s, but single young people are much less likely to attend church than single people of the previous generation. This problem is compounded by the trend that fewer people are getting married, and they are often older when they do. As a result, a key challenge for today's church is reaching young, single people.[11]

What Will Happen in the Future?

As you've probably figured out, there are a lot of good data about religion in the United States. This raises an intriguing possibility: Can we use this information to predict what will happen to Christianity in the future? The answer is absolutely yes, we can make predictions (and many people have). The real question is whether these predictions are accurate, and my answer is somewhere between maybe and probably not. There are so many factors that affect the size of a religion that it is difficult, if not impossible, to forecast each of them accurately. Among these factors are how many children members have, how long members live, how many members emigrate from other countries, how many people convert into the religion, and how many people leave the religion.

Think of it this way: Can you accurately predict who will win the Super Bowl next year? Do you know what will happen to a company's stock price? Can you always pick the winner of the reality television shows that you watch? Frankly, if you can answer yes to any of these questions, you have much more profitable things to do than read this book, but I'm guessing not. If we can't accurately forecast teams, companies, or shows, why do we think we can forecast religion, which is far larger and more complex?

Do you need more reason to be skeptical? Consider previous, failed predictions.[12]

• In 1761, Ezra Stiles, before he was president of Yale University, used demographic projection techniques to predict that in 100 years there would be 7 million Congregationalists and less than half a million Baptists. Turns out that, in fact, in 1860 there were 2 million Baptists and only half a million Congregationalists.

• In 1822, Thomas Jefferson predicted the imminent demise of Christianity in favor of Unitarianism. He wrote, "There is not a young man now living in the United States who will not die a Unitarian." He wasn't even close. Currently less than .5% of the population is Unitarian.

• In the 1800s, social theorist Auguste Comte stated that human society was outgrowing its "theological stage" of social evolution, and sociology would replace religion as the basis of moral judgment. (As someone who has spent twenty years in sociology, I am so, so glad that this did not happen.)

• In the 1800s, Frederich Engels predicted that a socialist revolution would cause religion to evaporate "soon."

Given my skepticism about predictions about the future of religion, I won't make any myself—there are already enough bad predictions out there. I will, however, review some predictions that have been made. I do this not so much because I think they are correct, but rather to illustrate how researchers think about religion.

A simple-minded approach to prediction is to assume that current trends will continue on into the future. Even if we don't know why a religion is changing, maybe we can assume that it will continue to change in the same way. The problem here is that social change rarely follows such a simple, linear path. For example, at the start of chapter 2, Figure 2.1 portrayed the percentage of religiously unaffiliated in the country. During the 1970s and 1980s, this number hovered around 6%. If we made a prediction at that point in time, we would have predicted a similarly low rate into the future. Then, however, during the 1990s, the percentage more than doubled, up to about 15%. Projecting that trend into the future, within twenty-five years there would not have been a single religious person in the country. Then, in this decade, the rate of increase has slowed considerably. Who knows what's next?

Here's a cartoon, from xkcd.com, that illustrates the pitfalls of using linear projections of the future.

Unfortunately, some people who make predictions do not give much detail about their reasoning, so their predictions are difficult to evaluate. These could be seat-of-the-pants guesses or simple extrapolations of current trends; we just don't know. What we do know is that they are largely negative:

- Pollster George Barna predicts that in twenty years only "one-third of the population will look to churches primarily or exclusively for experiencing their faith."[13]

- Michael Spencer, a commentator on church matters, wrote in the *Christian Science Monitor* that "within two generations, evangelicalism will be a house deserted of half its occupants."[14]

• David Olson, author of *The American Church in Crisis*, predicts that Christian church attendance rates will steadily drop such that by 2020 only 14.7% of the American population will attend a Christian church on a given weekend.[15]

• David Murrow, author of *Why Men Hate Going to Church*, predicts that the Christian church worldwide has at most 250 years before it is "totally overrun" by Islam and secularism.[16]

Another, more sophisticated approach to predictions is to model the various processes that make religions grow or shrink, such as fertility, conversions, and immigration. These predictions strike me as more thoughtful, but they are only as accurate as the assumptions they make. Interestingly, they tend to predict a more stable religious future than do the seat-of-the-pants predictions described above. Perhaps the most ambitious predictions are made by sociologist Erik Kaufmann.[17] He predicts that in the United States through 2043, the number of religiously unaffiliated will remain stable at its current levels, but there will be shuffling around among religions and denominations. The big winner will be Hispanic Catholics due to continued high levels of immigration. Conservative Protestants will drop a few percentage points in the coming decades as will non-Hispanic Catholics. In about a decade, Kaufmann predicts that the United States will have more Muslims than Jews.

So what conclusions can we draw? Christianity in the United States will grow, shrink, or stay about the same. We really have no idea. That said, there seems to be no compelling evidence—based on the data we have about our young people—that the church in America is on the verge of collapse.

CHAPTER 4

Are Evangelicals All Poor, Uneducated, Southern Whites?

Evangelicals are largely poor, uneducated, and easy to command.
—*Michael Weisskopf, Washington Post*

Why do men hate going to church?
—*David Murrow, Christian author*

The idiosyncrasies of history and geography cause Christianity to be expressed very differently in the . . . major regions of the country.
—*David Olson, The American Church in Crisis*

This chapter examines two related questions: Who is in the church? and How did they get there? To answer the first question, I will describe the personal characteristics of churchgoers, starting with the holy trinity of sociology—gender, race, and social class.

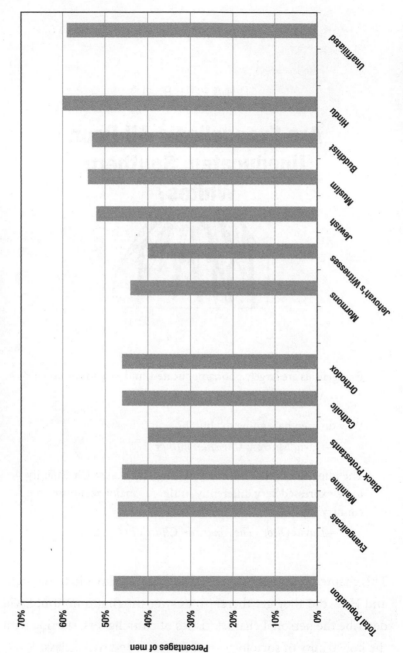

Figure 4.1: Gender Composition of Religions in the United States

Source: Pew U.S. Religious Landscape Survey, 2008

Gender

Regarding gender, it's a common perception that women are more religious than men. Is this true? Well, no and yes. In terms of religious affiliation, men are just about as likely to affiliate with religion as are women. Figure 4.1 graphs the percentage of men in the major religions in the United States. Forty-eight percent of survey respondents were men, and we see little difference with the major Christian groups—Evangelicals, Mainline Protestants, Orthodox, and Catholics—of whom 46 or 47% are men, though Black Protestants have only 40% male affiliation. Other world religions, in contrast, have higher rates of male adherents. Jews, Muslims, Hindus, and Buddhists each have more than 50% males. The two religious groups with the most men, Muslims and Hindus, are also comprised of many immigrants. This is no surprise, since immigrants are more likely to be men.[1] The religiously unaffiliated are also disproportionately male, with 59%.

But the real difference with gender occurs with religious beliefs and practices. Figure 4.2 graphs the gender difference among Evangelical Christians on various measures of participation, and women score substantially higher on every one of them. Evangelical women are more likely than men to think that religion is very important in their lives, to have an absolutely certain belief in a personal God, to attend church at least weekly, and to pray outside of religious services. Evangelical women are more active in their faith, and this seems to be why evangelical religious services attract more women. The prevalence of women in Christian practice is not a recent phenomenon. Historians have provided similar data for the 1800s, and they have estimated that church membership in the United States from the mid-1600s to the early 1800s was two-thirds female.[2]

This gender difference in religious practice has been defined as a significant problem for the church. In the book *Why Men Hate Going to Church*, David Murrow notes that 60% or more of attendees at

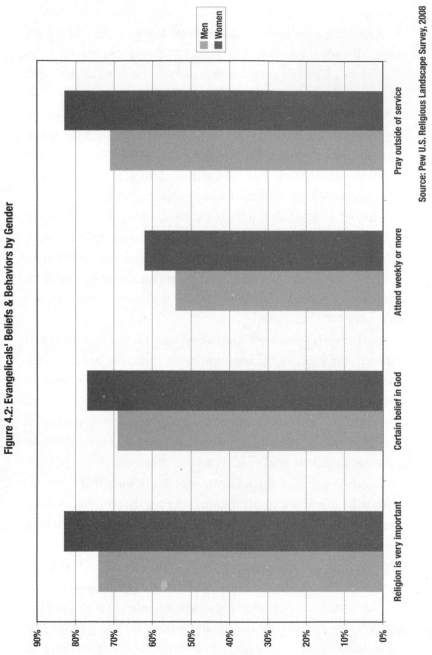

Figure 4.2: Evangelicals' Beliefs & Behaviors by Gender

Source: Pew U.S. Religious Landscape Survey, 2008

Christian church services are women, and he argues that Christian churches cater to women rather than men by creating a safe, quiet, female-oriented environment—one that calls for ceremony, control, and conformity. He offers various remedies to attract men by incorporating challenge, risk, and shorter sermons, making church more suitable to them.

Sociologist Rodney Stark, in his book *The Rise of Christianity*, argues that in fact the gender imbalance in Christianity might be one of its greatest assets, at least historically. He posits that the early Christian church grew quickly precisely because of its high number of female participants. Several factors worked to increase the number of women in the church. Christianity from the start prohibited infanticide—the killing of babies. This made an impression on women, since it was usually the girls, which were seen by society as less valuable, who were killed. The church also offered important benefits to women by prohibiting divorce, incest, marital infidelity, and polygamy. Christian women could marry later in life and have more of a choice in their marriage. Pagan women, in contrast, were sometimes forced into marriage before they even reached puberty.

Furthermore, according to Stark, as the church established a surplus of women, Christian women enjoyed higher social status, more power (at least within the church), and greater freedom. This, in turn, attracted even more women into the faith. Due to a dearth of Christian men, women would marry outside the church. This brought a steady stream of men into the church, because in a religiously mixed marriage, it was usually the less religious person who joined the religion of the more religious person.

The women of the early church also had relatively high fertility rates for that era. The Greco-Roman world had low fertility rates because it was a male culture that did not favor marriage. It also practiced infanticide, birth control, and abortion—the latter using crude and dangerous methods. Christians, in contrast, were commanded to "be fruitful and multiply." They placed a greater emphasis on marriage by emphasizing the obligations of the husband to the wife. They condemned promiscuity, and they prohibited abortion and infanticide—classifying them both as murder. Christian children grew up to be Christian adults, and so the high fertility rate of Christian women in the early church became a driving force in the rapid growth of the church overall.

In short, according to Stark, Christianity became a world religion by having a lot of women adherents.

Race

In a 1950s *Reader's Digest* article, Billy Graham lamented that eleven o'clock Sunday morning is the most racially segregated hour in America. This statement was repeated by Martin Luther King Jr. in his call for racial diversity within the Christian church.[3] Is the observation that religion is racially segregated still true? Unfortunately, yes, for the most part. An easy way to demonstrate this is to compare the racial composition of different religious traditions. If there were no segregation, they would have a similar racial makeup.

As shown in Figure 4.3, however, the racial composition of religions in America varies quite a bit. Here's how to interpret this chart: Each horizontal bar represents a different religious tradition (e.g., Evangelical Christians, Mainline Protestants, etc.). Each bar is divided up into different segments, represented by different shades, to indicate the racial makeup of that tradition. For reference, the top bar indicates that the general population is 71% White, 11% Black, 3% Asian, 3% other, and 11% Hispanic.

At a quick glance, we see substantial racial differences between groups. Jews are almost all White, while members of Black Protestant denominations, of course, are predominately, but not exclusively, African-American. Most of the religious traditions have mainly one or two

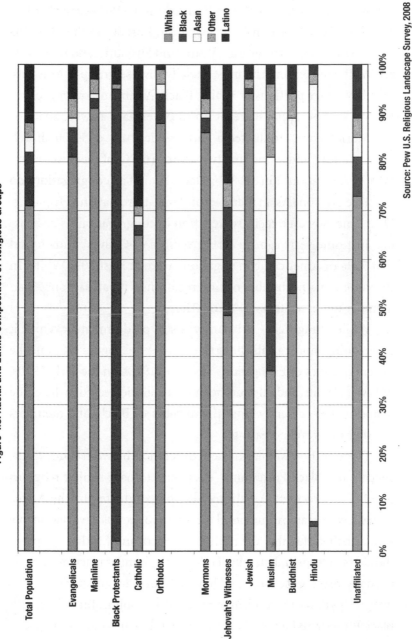

Figure 4.3: Racial and Ethnic Composition of Religious Groups

Source: Pew U.S. Religious Landscape Survey, 2008

83

racial and ethnic groups. Evangelicals, Mainline Protestants, Orthodox Christians, Mormons, and Jews are at least 80% White. Hindus are mostly Asian. Catholics are White and Hispanic, and Buddhists are White and Asian. The most racially diverse group is Muslims, who have large portions of White, Black, Asian, and other groups.

We see this racial segregation in other data as well. Sociologist Mark Chaves conducted a nationwide study of 1,500 church congregations and found that two-thirds (66%) of them were 80% White.[4] Also, about 1 in 8 is 80% Black. Half of all congregations do not have even one Asian member, and one-third have no Hispanics. Over time, however, racial segregation in congregations is decreasing. Just nine years ago, an earlier version of Chaves' study found that 72% of American congregations were at least 80% White. In the same vein, the number of congregations with at least one Asian member increased from 41% to 50%.

While evangelical Christianity is still predominately White, it is becoming more racially integrated over time. Figure 4.4 plots the racial identities of Evangelicals since the 1970s. In the early 1970s, 95% were White, and this number has steadily decreased each decade to about 80% currently. Both the number of Blacks and members of other races are increasing.

There are both similarities and differences between White Evangelicals and Black Protestants. They tend to have similar religious beliefs and practices. A nationwide poll conducted by the Angus Reid survey organization found that the two groups have reasonably similar beliefs: (1) that the Bible is inspired, and (2) that Scripture should be interpreted literally. They are also similar in terms of praying daily, reading the Bible, and having a born-again experience. The two groups differ, however, in their social and political attitudes, with Black Protestants being overall more liberal than White Evangelicals. For example, Black Protestants have had more faith in Democratic politicians, thought that the government should spend money on alleviating poverty, and had less trust in law-enforcement.[5]

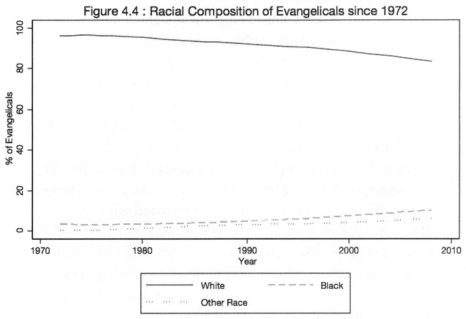

Figure 4.4 : Racial Composition of Evangelicals since 1972

Source : General Social Survey

Why the racial segregation in American Christianity? Some interpret this as racial discrimination. While discrimination undoubtedly exists throughout society, including the church, sociologists Michael Emerson and Christian Smith, in their book *Divided by Faith*, offer an alternative, and perhaps more compelling, explanation. They write that the organization of religion in America, and indeed much of what makes it so successful, inadvertently creates racial separation even when churches do not want to. Here is how it works. Generally speaking we're all more comfortable, at least initially, with people similar to us. This similarity can encompass many aspects of life, such as age, occupation, hobbies, education levels, and race. Not only are we more comfortable around people similar to ourselves, but social relations with similar people also tend to be more stable. Applied to religion, this means that people gravitate toward familiar churches with similar people, including people of the same race.

Furthermore, according to Emerson and Smith, people from different cultural backgrounds prefer different styles of religious worship and participation. For example, people from one racial group might prefer music with an upbeat tempo, whereas another group might prefer classic hymns. These preferences cover a wide range of church activities, including Sunday school, the length of the sermon, Communion, and liturgy. It's impossible for any one church to offer enough services to please everyone, so instead churches specialize in a particular style. This specialization allows them to become good at this approach, and it reduces costs, because the church doesn't have to have multiple specializations. The by-product of this specialization, however, is that any given religious style will attract a particular type of person. Given the significance of race and ethnicity in our country, this can result in racial sorting by congregations, denominations, and religions.

Emerson and Smith compare the Christian church to a large shopping mall. While malls have a few department stores that offer many different things for many people, most of their stores are highly specialized. There are clothing stores for pregnant women, video game stores for teenage boys, home décor shops for homeowners, Disney stores for kids, and electronic gadget stores for middle-aged sociologists. It's difficult for any one store to appeal to everyone, so stores prosper by specializing. This same dynamic, according to Emerson and Smith, is at play in churches. To be successful, most churches have to specialize, and this, in turn, results in similarity among its members among various dimensions, including race.

In short, racial separation occurs as the unintended, and often unwanted, by-product of the very things that make churches strong.

Class

A final characteristic that I'll cover is social class. Sociologists spend a lot of time researching class, and there are multiple, sometimes highly technical, definitions of it. For our purposes, let's just say that social class refers to a person's relative social and economic status in society. People with more social class have more money, fame, and power. One measure of social class is education, for people with more education tend to make more money, to have more career opportunities, and overall to be held in higher esteem than those without.

A common stereotype about Evangelical Christians is that we are poor and uneducated. (After spending fourteen years in college, grad school, and a post-doctorate, I certainly fit one of those two characteristics.) An infamous *Washington Post* article about Evangelical Christians referred to them as poor, undereducated, and easily led.[6] Granted, this is an extreme example, but critiques of Christianity in America, especially of Evangelicals, often have an underlying theme that Christianity is incongruent with a proper education.

Figure 4.5 describes the college graduation rates of different religious groups. Nationwide, 27% of all adults have graduated from college. Hindus, Jews, Buddhists, and Orthodox Christians have the highest levels of education. Catholics, Mormons, and Muslims are at about the national average, and Jehovah's Witnesses have by far the lowest education. Evangelicals are somewhat below the national average. The religiously unaffiliated are just slightly above average in levels of college education. The irony is that some of the religiously unaffiliated explain their rejection of religion in terms of superior learning, but several religious groups have much higher levels of education.

Many people assume that going to college diminishes beliefs, because in college one learns about other belief systems and is exposed to people from a wide range of backgrounds. Among the general population, this diminishing is to some extent supported by the data.

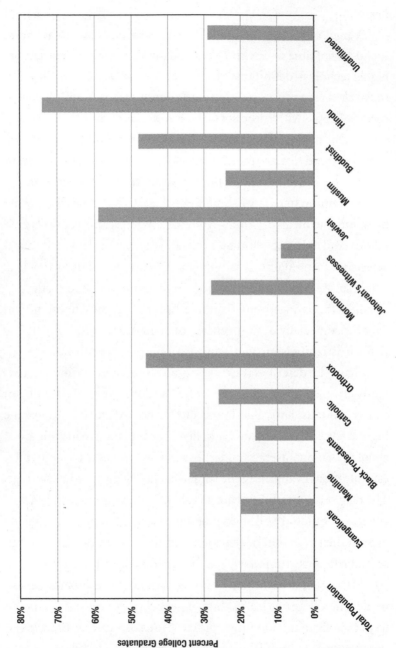

Figure 4.5: College Graduation Rates by Religious Group

Percent College Graduates

Source: Pew U.S. Religious Landscape Survey, 2008

According to the Pew Religious Landscape Survey, 60% of high school graduates who didn't go to college view religion as very important. These numbers go down to 55% of those with some college education and 50% of college graduates. A similar pattern holds true with a certainty in God and praying outside of religious services (although there are little differences in church attendance rates by education).

A very different story emerges, however, for Evangelicals. Among them, increased education is associated with more, rather than less, religiousness. As shown in Figure 4.6, Evangelical Christians who graduated from college are slightly more likely to think that religion is very important. The most educated Evangelicals are also more certain in their belief in God, attend religious services more frequently, and pray more often outside of religious services.[7]

How would we explain this counterintuitive finding? Sociologist Christian Smith presents an interesting theory.[8] According to Smith, Evangelicals define themselves and their faith, in part, by being different from their surrounding society. Cultural conflict strengthens Evangelicals' faith, and what better way to experience this conflict than college? Going to college causes Evangelicals to further engage society, thus highlighting and strengthening their faith. In contrast, some religious groups seek to isolate themselves from conventional society. For these groups, education may weaken their faith.

Evangelical parents worry about the faith of their children, and understandably so. For some, this leads to attempts to shelter the child from "secular" society and its various religious perspectives. Ironically, however, engaging society might actually be the best way for Evangelicals to strengthen their faith. Evangelical parents: Do you want your child to stay with the faith? Perhaps one of the best things you can do is make sure he or she is well-educated. At the very least, sending your children off to college is not necessarily something to fear (at least for their faith—for your finances, yes, run away screaming).

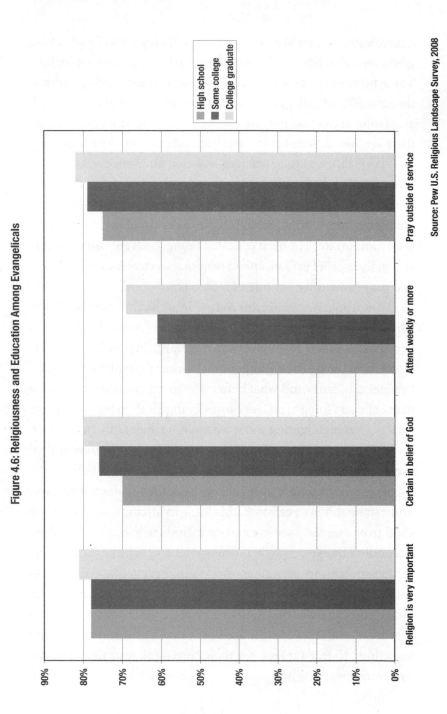

Figure 4.6: Religiousness and Education Among Evangelicals

Source: Pew U.S. Religious Landscape Survey, 2008

The Geography of Religion

Let's transition now from talking about the personal characteristics of Evangelicals to their geographical distribution. The United States is thought of as a religious country, and rightfully so; however, this doesn't mean that religion is spread equally over the map, as regions of the country vary in both the amount and type of religion practiced. Figure 4.7 is a map of all the counties in the United States, and each county is shaded to indicate the percentage of its residents who adhere to any religion.[9] The darker the shade, the higher the percentage of religious adherence. As shown, there is wide variation from region to region. The most religious part of the country is the middle third. In this area, encompassing the Great Plains, the Midwest, and part of the South, more than half the residents of most counties adhere to a religion. The least religious section is the far West. Except for Mormon Utah, most counties west of the Rocky Mountains have relatively low rates of religious adherence. The East Coast is a mixture, with pockets of low and high rates of adherence scattered throughout.

Americans vary not only in whether they adhere to religion by geography but also which religious denominations they belong to. The American religious landscape is dominated by Baptists and Catholics. Baptists constitute a majority in almost every county in the South—between Texas and the Atlantic Ocean, and between the Gulf of Mexico and southern Indiana. If you found yourself in the middle of this area, say northern Mississippi, you'd have to drive a long way before you stopped seeing a lot of Baptist churches. In contrast to Baptists, who are concentrated in the South, Catholics are spread throughout the country. Most of the non-Mormon counties in the West have more Catholics than any other single group. This is also true in New England, the upper industrial states, lower Texas, and the Florida Coast. Lutherans are concentrated in the Dakotas and Minnesota. In fact, researchers have observed that the number

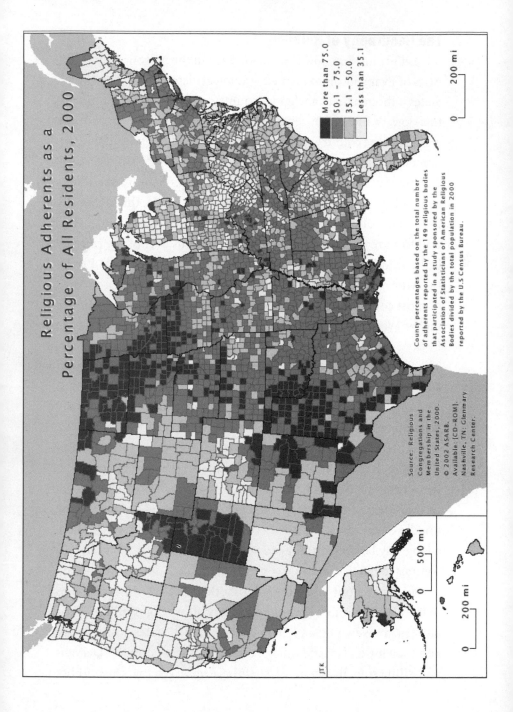

Religious Adherents as a
Percentage of All Residents, 2000

More than 75.0
50.1 – 75.0
35.1 – 50.0
Less than 35.1

0   200 mi

Source: Religious
Congregations and
Membership in the
United States, 2000.
© 2002 ASARB.
Available: (CD–ROM).
Nashville, TN: Glenmary
Research Center.

County percentages based on the total number
of adherents reported by the 149 religious bodies
that participated in a study sponsored by the
Association of Statisticians of American Religious
Bodies divided by the total population in 2000
reported by the U.S Census Bureau.

0   500 mi

0   200 mi

JTK

of Lutherans in a given area steadily decreases with its distance from the North Dakota-Minnesota borders.[10] Methodist counties span horizontally from Maryland to Colorado, and Mormon counties are found mostly in Utah and bordering states.

The distribution of religious affiliation in the United States is the result of its history, with a special emphasis on, of all things, mountain ranges.[11] The colonial-era churches on the East Coast were predominately Anglican and Congregationalist. However, as the pioneers started moving west, they encountered the Appalachian Mountains, which made life rougher. For the most part, it was not the more settled Anglicans and Congregationalists who pioneered the frontier but the newly emerging Methodists and Baptists. The routes of the Methodist circuit riders are reflected in the concentration of Methodist churches across the middle of the country. Below that are Baptists. Later, Lutheran immigrants, originally from Northern Europe, settled in New York, New Jersey, and Pennsylvania. From there they moved west across the Upper Midwest to their current homeland, Lake Wobegon. Roman Catholics, many of whom were immigrants, settled in the large industrial cities throughout the East and the Midwest. Going farther west, pioneers eventually encountered the Rocky Mountains, which proved such a formidable obstacle that few of the Midwestern religious groups crossed them. Instead, the religions west of the Rockies tend to be homegrown Christian and Mormon groups as well as Catholic Hispanics. Just think: What if the mountain ranges in the Continental United States ran East-West instead of North-South? We might all be Episcopalians and Congregationalists.

Regarding Evangelicals, the South has many, with its high concentration of Baptists. But what about the rest of the country? Are Evangelicals losing whole regions? For instance, a recent study labeled New England to be the "new stronghold of the religiously unidentified." In response to this study, R. Albert Mohler Jr, president

93

of the Southern Baptist Theological Seminary, lamented this change by stating that the Northeast was an early stronghold of American religion, so to lose it "struck me as momentous."[12]

To examine the regional distribution of Evangelicals, I calculated their percentage in four different regions—West, Midwest, East, and South. As shown in Figure 4.8, the South has a much greater concentration of Evangelicals than the other regions. Currently, more than one-third of all southern adults affiliate as Evangelicals. Far fewer easterners—only about 1 in 10—are Evangelicals. The West and the Midwest are in-between these extremes.

Over time the South has seen a slow but steady decline in the percentage of Evangelicals, dropping from about 40% in the 1970s to about 35% currently. In contrast, the East has seen an increase, from 6 to 11%. This increase in eastern Evangelicals has helped to offset the decrease of southern Evangelicals. Both the West and the Midwest witnessed an increase in the percentage of Evangelicals from the 1970s to the 1980s and a decrease from the 1990s to the present. Over time, the difference in Evangelical rates between regions is decreasing. If you're familiar with statistics, this change represents an instance of "regression to the mean"—more extreme scores become less so over time. If this trend continues, and who knows if it will, then in the future the distribution of Evangelicals will be more uniform throughout the country.

Historian Mark Noll highlights an implication of the geographical concentration of Evangelicals in the South. He writes that the nation's elite educational institutions and media centers are concentrated in the Northeast and the West, and these are regions with comparatively fewer Evangelicals. This means that academics and journalists have relatively fewer interactions with Evangelicals, and this can lead to their having misapprehensions about them.[13]

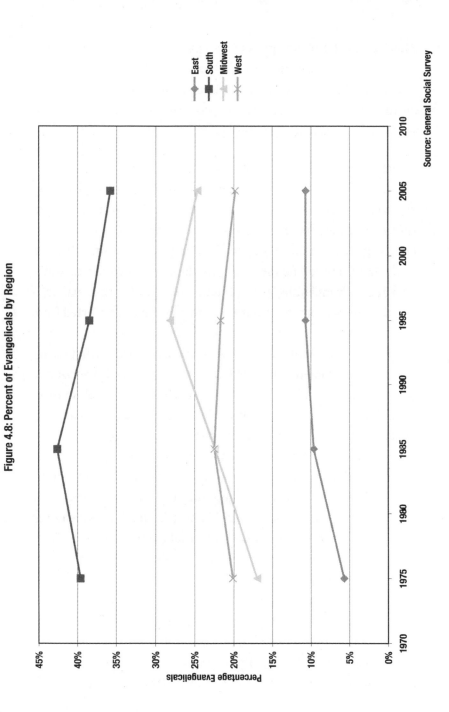

Figure 4.8: Percent of Evangelicals by Region

Source: General Social Survey

The Dynamics of Religious Change

Let's move from talking about who Christians are to how they got to be Christians in the first place. That is, sometimes people switch between religions. This raises questions about where Christians come from and where they go.

Where Do Members Come From?

In evangelical churches, there is considerable emphasis on evangelism—bringing non-Christians to faith; and this is often spoken of as the primary mechanism of church growth. In addition, church growth is affected by fertility rates and keeping children in the faith. This being the case, a fundamental sociological question about Evangelicals, and about any religion for that matter, is whether its members were born into that group or converted from another group.

Figure 4.9 presents data that addresses this question. In this figure, reporting data from the 2008 Landscape Survey, each horizontal bar represents a different religious group. The lighter colored section, on the left of each bar, represents the percentage of that group raised in that religion. The darker section, on the right, represents the percentage of people who switched over to that group after being raised in a different group. As you can see, religious groups in the United States vary widely in where they get their members. Over 80% of Protestant, Catholic, Jewish, and Hindu adults were raised as such. In contrast, more than half of Jehovah's Witnesses, Buddhists, and the religiously unaffiliated were raised in other groups and switched over later in life.

From the same Pew study we can analyze various Protestant groups in more detail. Surprisingly, only about one-half of evangelical adults were raised in an evangelical church. Another 30% were raised in the Mainline Protestant or Historically Black tradition. About 10% were raised as Catholics (the category in which

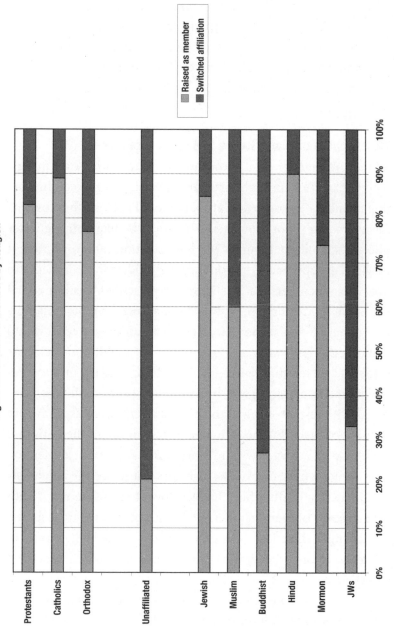

Figure 4.9: Sources of Members by Religion

I fall). Only 2% were raised in a non-Christian religion, and 6% were raised unaffiliated to any particular religion. As such, the great majority of Evangelical Christians were brought up in a Christian home, though not necessarily an evangelical home. Conversions, especially from other religions, account for a relatively small number of Evangelicals.

What Happens to People Raised in Religious Traditions?

For a religious group to grow, it has to both bring in new members, either through birth or conversion, and keep its current members. A group that attracts a lot of converts but loses its members might not grow at all—it would be like pouring water into a leaky bucket. Figure 4.10 plots retention rates for different religious groups, and as shown they vary widely in their ability to hold on to members. Each religion is represented by a horizontal bar divided into three sections. The first section represents how many members raised in that religious tradition stayed in it into adulthood. The next section represents the childhood members who switched to a different religious tradition, and the final section represents the members who became religiously unaffiliated. Hindus and Protestants showed the highest retention rates, with 80% or more of their childhood members remaining in the faith into adulthood. Catholics, Jews, and Mormons have mid-range retention rates, ranging from 68 to 76%. Jehovah's Witnesses, the religiously unaffiliated, and Buddhists had the lowest retention rates, with 50% or fewer of their members remaining in that religious group. Interestingly, these last three groups also had the highest rates of conversion from other groups—suggesting that their membership is very fluid.

As shown in the graph, the religiously unaffiliated show low levels of retention, but this might be changing over time. The data shown here are from a cross section of adults, and so it compounds

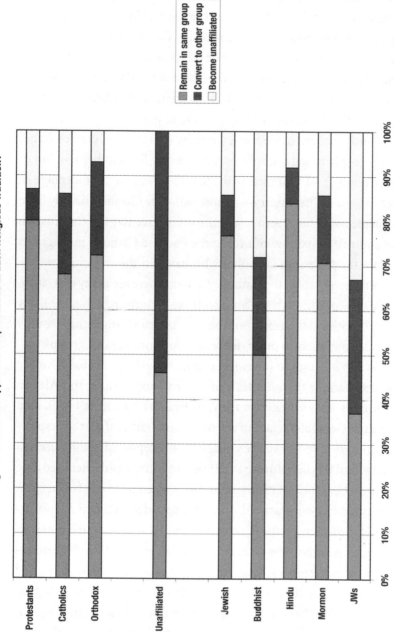

Figure 4.10: What Happens to People Raised in Each Religious Tradition?

Source: Pew U.S. Religious Landscape Survey, 2008

the experiences of both young and old. More detailed analysis of the religiously unaffiliated has found that earlier in the twentieth century, it was common for people raised without a religious affiliation to convert to a religion in adulthood, typically upon marriage. In more recent decades, however, this pattern has changed. Now those raised without religion are as likely to remain unaffiliated as those raised with religion are to stay in their religion.[14]

Much has been made about the retention rates of Catholics. About 1 in 3 people raised Catholic end up leaving for another religion or no religion at all. Coupled with this outflow, a high percentage of immigrants to this country—almost half—are Catholic, usually from Hispanic countries.[15] As a result, the total percentage of Catholics in the country remains about the same because Catholic immigrants replace the American Catholics who have left the church; however, given the large size of the Catholic Church, there are many ex-Catholics in our country. When Catholics leave their church, they are likely to join another denomination, and so American Catholicism steadily provides members to other denominations or religious groups.

When it comes to retention rates, Evangelicals probably worry the most about the retention of their young people. In order to document what actually happens to Evangelical youth, I took data from the General Social Survey of respondents. Of all the respondents interviewed since the year 2000, 409 reported being raised in Evangelical families during the 1990s. In other words, here are data about 409 Evangelical youth in the 1990s who are now between eighteen and thirty-six years old. So what happened to them? As it turns out, 74% of these Evangelical kids' families remained Evangelicals as adults. Another 7% switched to another Christian denomination, mostly becoming Mainline Protestants. Three percent joined other, non-Christian religions, and 16% disaffiliated from religion altogether. Whether this retention rate of Evangelical youth is high or low is a matter of interpretation, and it could be argued both ways:

Is the glass half full, or has the water already been spilled? However, the recent experiences of Evangelical youth show no indication of the immediate collapse of Evangelical Christianity in the United States. Furthermore, since people generally become more religious as they age, it's possible that some of these people who left their Evangelical roots will return as they enter into mid-life.

To understand religion in America, we must know about the migration rates in and out of any religious group. Figure 4.11 is a really cool figure that I have borrowed from Michael Bell, who writes for the blog *eclecticchristian.com*.[16] It's a little complex, but it's worth taking the time to figure out. The data come from the Pew U.S. Religious Landscape Survey of 2008, the same data that I've reported in the past two Figures. The top bar of the graph represents the childhood faith group of respondents in the recent Pew Study. The wider the segment, the more people were raised in that religious group. The bottom bar is the current faith group of respondents, at the time of the interview. The lines between them show where people go. For example, the current bar for the "none" group, i.e., the religiously unaffiliated, is wider than the childhood bar, indicating that this group has grown over time. The lines going out of childhood "nones" indicate what happens to people raised without religious affiliation. About half stay unaffiliated, and among the other half, the biggest portion goes to the Evangelical church. The lines going into the current "none" bar vary in thickness. The thickest line comes from childhood Catholics, indicating that a sizable portion of currently unaffiliated people were raised Catholic. Thick lines also come from childhood "nones" and Evangelicals. There's a lot of cool information in this graph, and it looks even better in color, if you want to look it up on the Web (the link is provided in the endnotes).[17] I won't review all the information here other than to point out that this graph, perhaps more than any other presentation I've seen, demonstrates the fluid nature of religion in the United States.

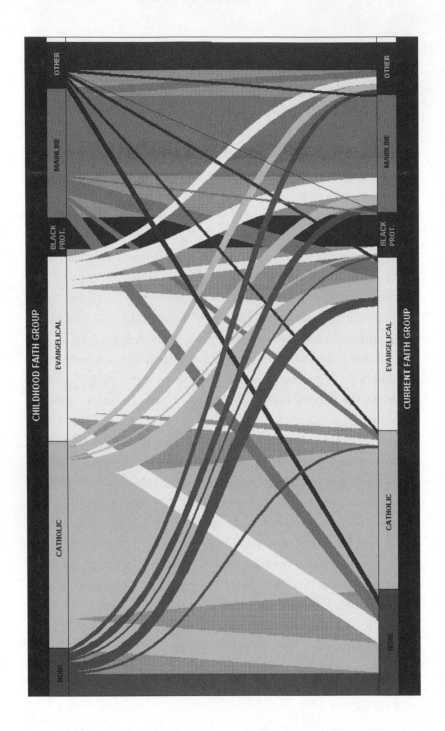

CHILDHOOD FAITH GROUP

OTHER · MAINLINE · BLACK PROT. · EVANGELICAL · CATHOLIC · NONE

CURRENT FAITH GROUP

OTHER · MAINLINE · BLACK PROT. · EVANGELICAL · CATHOLIC · NONE

CHAPTER 5

Do Christians Think and Do Christian Things?

Evangelicals desperately need moral and spiritual renewal—on that everyone agrees.

—*Cover of a major evangelical Christian magazine*

The behavior and attitudes of the great mass of Evangelicals aren't what we think they are.

—*Christine Wicker, The Fall of the Evangelical Nation.*

Only 9% of born-again Christians have a biblical worldview.

—*George Barna*[1]

Another fear message about Christians goes something like this: "Well, if there still are Christians in the United States, they certainly don't have proper Christian beliefs and actions, especially when compared to the Christians of the past." According to this message, today's Christians are watered down, both in what they believe and what they do.

This message is a central theme in the research of George Barna and the Barna Research Group. For example, their 2007 Annual Tracking Report concluded that since 1984, "commitment to orthodox biblical perspectives is slipping in a number of areas."[2] In his book *Revolution*, Barna also writes of the Christian faith in America as "relatively compromised and complacent."[3] In a recent study, the Barna Group summarized that "Christians have a diverse set of beliefs—but many of those beliefs are contradictory, or at least inconsistent."[4]

Barna isn't the only one sounding this message. For example, a recent article from the Christian Broadcasting Network (CBN) laments American Christians' lack of knowledge about the Bible.[5] The story starts with the bold claim that "Some Christian leaders say this generation is the most biblically illiterate in history" (though no specific attributions are made). I'm not sure what to make of this, since literacy is a relatively recent phenomenon, at least in historical terms.[6] Many generations could not read anything, let alone the Bible. Nonetheless, the article goes on to defend this claim by describing how its author went to a beach and asked several young people questions, such as about the Ten Commandments. Lo and behold, it turns out that some of the young beachgoers didn't know much about the Bible.

To get a better sense of Evangelicals' religious practices, this chapter examines four aspects of religious life: beliefs, practices, commitment, and experiences. It compares Evangelicals to other religions and denominations, and then, when suitable data are available, analyzes if Evangelicals have changed in recent decades.[7]

Central Beliefs

Perhaps the most basic question regarding religion is whether someone believes in God (or a Universal Spirit, for some religions). Since most Americans do believe in God, survey questions also ask about people's certainty in their beliefs. Figure 5.1 reports the percentage of people in different religions who are "absolutely certain" of the

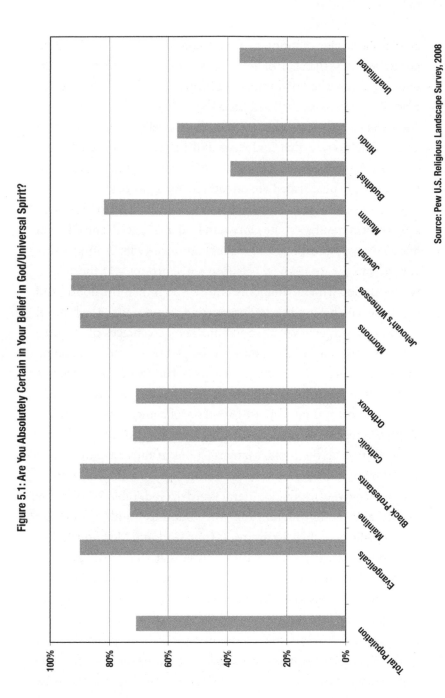

Figure 5.1: Are You Absolutely Certain in Your Belief in God/Universal Spirit?

Source: Pew U.S. Religious Landscape Survey, 2008

existence of a God. As shown, there is considerable variation across groups, with less than half of Jews and Buddhists being absolutely certain about God, and 90% or more of Mormons, Jehovah's Witnesses, Black Protestants, and Evangelicals. Most of the rest of Evangelicals are "fairly certain" about God. Over a third of the religiously unaffiliated are absolutely certain that God exists, and, in fact, 70% of them believe in God at some level of certainty (this highlights, again, that many of the religiously unaffiliated are not atheists or agnostics).

How has Evangelicals' belief in God changed over time? Is there a downward trend, as some Christian leaders suggest? The General Social Survey has explored this question since 1988. From the survey, we can divide Evangelicals into three groups: (1) those who believe in God with no doubts, (2) those who sometimes doubt, and (3) those who believe in a higher power (as opposed to the biblical God) or do not believe in God at all. The percentages of all three groups have remained the same over the past two decades, revealing that Evangelicals' certainty in God does not appear to be in decline. Throughout this time period, about 80% of Evangelicals believe in God without any doubt, about 15% report having some doubt, and about 5% report believing in a higher power or no God at all.

Let's turn to the Bible. Many religious groups have their own sacred texts, and they vary in the extent to which they view these texts as being the inspired or literal Word of God. Table 5.2 plots the scriptural views of different religions. Buddhists and Jews are the least likely to view their scriptures as from God, and Mormons, Jehovah's Witnesses, and Evangelical Christians are the most likely.

Those respondents who believe that the Bible is the Word of God could take this to mean one of two things. They might say that the Bible is the literal Word of God (i.e., it is to be taken as absolute truth, word-for-word), or they might say it is the inspired Word of God (i.e., not everything is word-for-word from God, but the Bible is still inspired by God). Among Evangelical Christians, 59% view

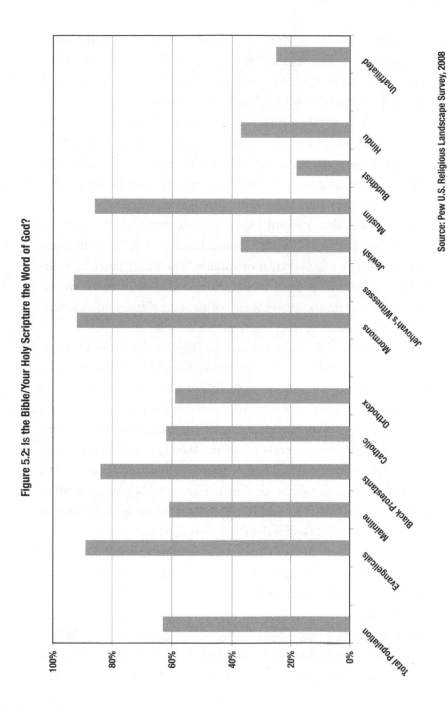

Figure 5.2: Is the Bible/Your Holy Scripture the Word of God?

Source: Pew U.S. Religious Landscape Survey, 2008

the Bible as the literal Word of God, and 30% view it as the Word of God but not literally so. Seven percent of Evangelicals think the Bible was simply written by men and is not the Word of God, and 5% don't know. Likewise, 62% of Black Protestants take a literal view of the Bible. In contrast, only 22% of Mainline Protestants and 23% of Catholics adopt a word-for-word interpretation of Scripture.

It is no surprise that Evangelicals take Scripture so seriously, for it is one of our defining characteristics. Recently several well-known Evangelicals, including author Os Guinness, philosopher Dallas Willard, and seminary president Richard Mouw, put together what they call "An Evangelical Manifesto." In it they state the need to define Evangelical identity in light of a particular orientation toward Scripture.[8] Specifically: "We believe that Jesus' own teaching and his attitude toward the total truthfulness and supreme authority of the Bible, God's inspired Word, make the Scriptures our final rule for faith and practice."

Evangelicals' attitudes toward the Bible have changed little in recent years. The General Social Survey has plotted these attitudes since the mid-1980s. Few Evangelical Christians think of the Bible as a book of man-made fables, and this number has remained very low, below 10%, since the survey began. The remainder of Evangelicals hold the Bible as the literal or inspired Word of God. In the 1980s, the portion viewing it as literal dropped from its high point of just over 60%, while those viewing it as inspired rose. But it's been rather steady since about 1990, with about 55% of Evangelicals holding to the literal Word of God and 40% the inspired Word.

Another core belief of Christianity is life after death. According to Pew research, among Christians, Evangelicals have the highest rates of believing in the afterlife, at 86%. The other Christian groups range from 74% to 79% of those who believe in the afterlife. Among other religions, a remarkably high number of Mormons—98%—believe in the afterlife. Now, I'm not sure who the remaining 2% of Mormons are, but I think they might be in trouble. At the other end of the spectrum, fewer than half of Jews, Jehovah's Witnesses, and the religiously unaffiliated believe in life after death.

There are many other theological beliefs in the Christian faith. The General Social Survey has asked about some of these, and Table 5.3 indicates the portion of Evangelicals who believe in heaven, hell, miracles, and angels. In every instance, over 80% but fewer than 90% of Evangelicals affirmed these ideas. Understandably, church leaders would like these numbers to be at 100%, but there isn't the rampant disbelief in these topics that one might expect, given popular discussions about them by Evangelicals.

Table 5.3: How Many Evangelicals Believe in _____?

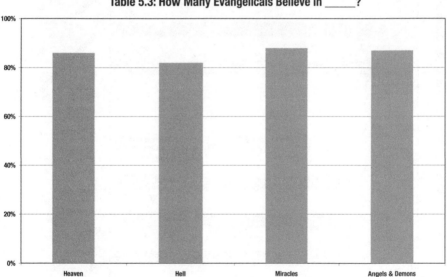

Another way to think about religious beliefs is in terms of absolute truth. Figure 5.4 graphs how many people believe that there are clear and absolute standards for what is right and wrong. Here we see more agreement across religions, for over half of each religious group represented believed in absolute standards, but no group has more than 90% agreeing with this. Among Christians, Evangelicals had the highest percentage at 84%. The other Christian traditions

109

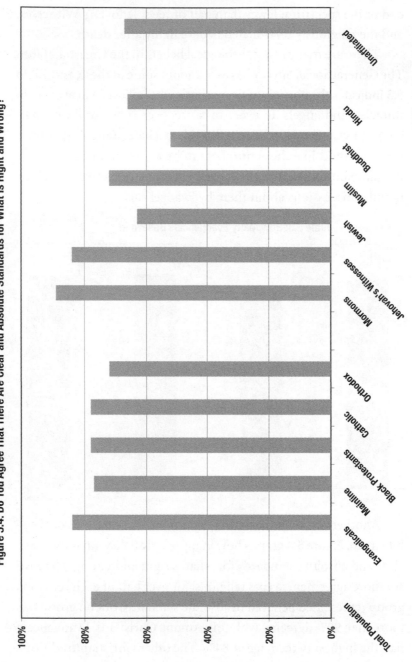

Figure 5.4: Do You Agree That There Are Clear and Absolute Standards for What Is Right and Wrong?

Source: Pew U.S. Religious Landscape Survey, 2008

ranged from 72 to 78%. Among other religions, Mormons and Jehovah's Witnesses had the highest rates of belief, and Buddhists, Jews, and Hindus had the lowest. Somewhat surprisingly, two-thirds of the religiously unaffiliated believe in absolute truth, indicating that in fact they are not all postmodern, secular humanists who believe in relative truth, as is often assumed by Christians. Once again, conventional wisdom seems to be wrong.

Importance of Religion

Another way of gauging people's religious faith is to ask them how important religion is to them. In our churches, we all know people who take their faith seriously and those who don't, and it seems that Christian pastors spend a lot of time and energy trying to move people from the latter group to the former. Does the importance of one's religion vary across religions? In other words, do some groups take their beliefs more seriously than others? According to the data, the answer is yes. When asked the question "How important is religion in your life?" over three-quarters of Evangelicals and Black Protestants answered "very important." However, only about half of the other Christian groups—Mainline Protestants, Catholics, and Orthodox Christians—hold religion as very important. Among other religions, Jehovah's Witnesses and Mormons were the most likely to answer "very important," whereas far fewer Jews, Buddhists, and Hindus answered the same. As we might expect, very few of the religiously unaffiliated, only 16%, stated that religion was "very important."

Prayer and Scripture

The analyses in this chapter so far have focused on what people believe and value, and that's certainly an essential aspect of religion, but there are also religious activities. In other words, do people's actions follow their beliefs? Presumably, the people who strongly hold religious beliefs also practice religious activities the most often, but this is not necessarily the case, so it's worth exploring. Religions have many activities associated with them, so I will start with two of the most basic ones: prayer and reading Scripture. Even if everyone in a religion prays, which is probably not the case, some certainly pray more than others. Likewise, some people read Scripture more often. Figure 5.5 examines how many people, outside of religious services, pray on a daily basis or read Scripture on a weekly basis (or more often). Several patterns emerge in this figure. In every religious tradition, more people pray on a daily basis than read Scripture on a weekly basis. Also, those religions in which people pray the most tend to have the highest rates of Scripture reading. Among Christians, about 80% of Evangelicals and Black Protestants pray daily, and 60% read Scripture at least weekly. In contrast, only 50 to 60% of Mainline Protestants, Catholics, and Orthodox Christians pray daily, and about a quarter or less read Scripture daily.

Among other religions, Mormons and Jehovah's Witnesses log the highest rates of daily prayer and weekly Scripture reading, hovering around 80% for both. Hindus, Buddhists, and especially Jews, record low levels of prayer and Scripture reading.

What would probably surprise many outspoken Christian leaders is the fact that over time, Evangelicals are praying more often. For the last three decades, the General Social Survey has asked Evangelicals if they pray on a daily basis. In the 1980s and 1990s, about two-thirds of Evangelicals prayed daily, but in this decade the number has risen to three-quarters. I'm not sure why prayer activity has increased, but it is good news for the Evangelical church. Just a thought—maybe they are praying that church leaders will be more careful in using statistics?

Unfortunately, there were only two years in which the General Social Survey asked respondents how often they read Scripture: 1988 and 1998. While far from conclusive, these two data points show roughly stable Bible reading rates at those two points in time, with about half of Evangelicals reading their Bible on at least a weekly basis.

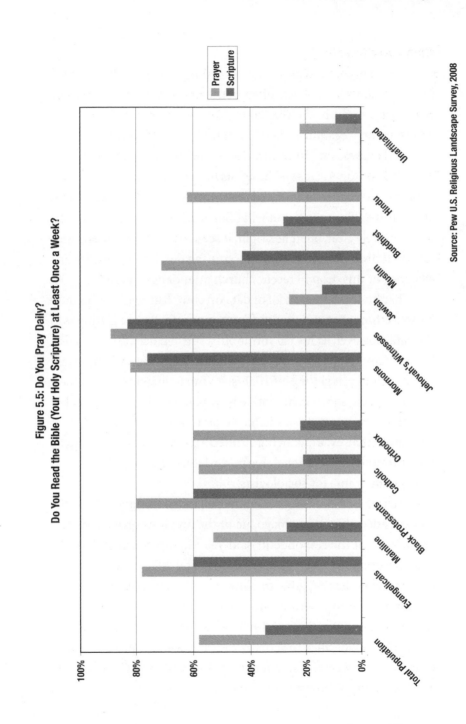

Figure 5.5: Do You Pray Daily?
Do You Read the Bible (Your Holy Scripture) at Least Once a Week?

Source: Pew U.S. Religious Landscape Survey, 2008

Going to Church

Christians go to church, but according to George Barna, they will go to church much less often in the near future. In *Revolution*, Barna writes that in the year 2000, 70% of Americans had a local religious congregation as their "primary means of spiritual experience and expression." In contrast, according to his prediction, only 30 to 35% of Americans will have this in the year 2025. The rest will focus on alternative faith-based communities and the media, arts, and culture.[9] The specifics of what Barna means by this prediction aren't entirely clear, but if he's right, it seems that church attendance rates will drop precipitously in the coming decades. Do we see any evidence of this drop in recent church attendance trends?

Thankfully, there are a lot of data on church attendance because it's something that sociologists like to measure. Before getting into the data, however, let me tell you about a spirited debate sociologists have had about measuring church attendance.[10] Now, when we talk about sociologists getting into fights, it's fun to imagine guys in their fifties, wearing sports coats with elbow patches, throwing punches at each other—a nerdy, academic version of a cage match. Alas, it isn't quite that exciting, being limited to debates in the research literature and the occasional sharp word during a presentation. But this is high drama for sociologists.

Starting in the 1930s, the Gallup Poll asked respondents if they had attended church or synagogue in the previous seven days, and about 40% of the respondents said yes. Gallup continued asking this question, and over the decades, a steady 40% or so of Americans reported having gone to church in the previous week. This percentage number became an article of faith among researchers (pun intended) until the mid-1990s, when researcher Kirk Hadaway and colleagues decided to actually count how many people went to church.[11] They went to Catholic churches in Ashtabula County, Ohio, and they counted how many people showed up for church services over a several-month period. They found that 24% of the Catholics in the county were in church each week. Then they did a traditional phone survey and found that 51% of Catholic respondents said that they had gone to church in the prior week. They termed the difference between actual and reported attendance as the "overstatement gap." Based on their study of Ashtabula County, Hadaway and friends estimated this gap to be about 100%—meaning that Christians reported double their actual church attendance rates.

Some researchers agree with Hadaway and his colleagues' claim, others don't, believing that they, ironically, exaggerate how much Christians exaggerate. My own impression of the literature is that there is some overstatement, but not as much as Hadaway and his coauthors claim. My views tend toward those of sociologists Claude Fischer and Michael Hout, who write that "The survey-based estimate of church attendance is probably 10 to 30% too high as a measure of a typical Sunday's congregations."[12]

Some researchers posit that Christians overstate their church attendance to look good for researchers. This explanation doesn't resonate with me because I don't know why Christians would think that researchers would be impressed with weekly church attendance. Based on my own experiences as a Christian churchgoer, I find two other explanations more compelling. Although the survey asks Christians if they attended church in the previous week, this could be interpreted by the respondent as meaning do you *intend* to go to church every week? They might answer yes, even though they don't actually go every week, since things come up sometimes, like getting sick or a kid's soccer tournament. Another explanation is that the survey question could be measuring something other than Sunday services. Researchers have focused on Sunday morning services, but many churches have worship services at other times, and there are also other forms of meetings. As such, someone who says they go to church every week may also be counting going to a weekly Bible study or an informal meeting with friends at church.

For the purposes of this book, I'm going to assume that over-statement rates regarding church attendance remain mostly stable over time, and so we can observe whether attendance rates are going up or down over time, even if we don't know the exact rates in any given year.[13] Let's start by comparing Evangelicals to other denominations and religions. According to the research, among Christian groups, Evangelicals and Black Protestants have similarly high weekly attendance rates, just below 60%, which is substantially higher than other Protestants, Catholics, or Orthodox Christians. Among other religious groups, Jehovah's Witnesses and Mormons have very high attendance rates, with three out of four members or more attending religious services each week. The lowest attendance rates, fewer than 1 in 4 attending weekly, are among the unaffiliated, Jews, Buddhists, and Hindus.[14]

If we look at how this has changed over time, there is little evidence that church attendance rates among Evangelicals are decreasing; in fact, they may even be increasing. The General Social Survey asks: "How often do you attend religious services?" Respondents' answers are coded into nine categories, ranging from "never" to "several times a week." For ease of presentation, I've collapsed respondents into 1 of 4 groups: Those who attend nearly every week, those who attend at least once a month, those who attend at least once a year, and those who attend less often (including never). Figure 5.6 plots the percentage of Evangelicals who have fit into each of these categories since the early 1970s, and as shown, Evangelicals' rates of church attendance remained mostly stable into the 1990s. At that point, however, they trended upward, with an increased percentage of Evangelicals attending church on a weekly basis. Similarly, the percentage of Evangelicals who attended church on only a yearly basis declined during that time period.

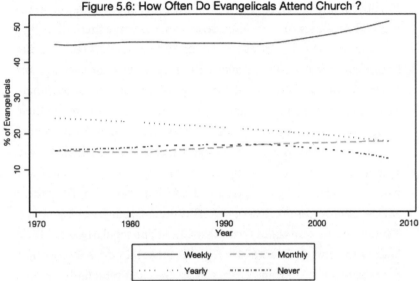

Figure 5.6: How Often Do Evangelicals Attend Church ?

Source : General Social Survey

How might we explain this apparent increase in church attendance among Evangelicals? One possibility is that it mirrors the increased number of religiously unaffiliated during the same period. As you might remember, way back in chapter 2, the number of religiously unaffiliated Americans increased substantially in the 1990s. Those most likely to leave Christianity included those who were not strongly attached to the church in the first place. This being the case, it seems reasonable to assume that the departure of less-committed Evangelicals would leave behind a higher percentage of more-committed Evangelicals, who would evidence more frequent rates of attending church.

Commitment to Mission

In addition to whether Christians attend church, we can also examine how involved they are in the mission of the church. This has various manifestations and one of them—obviously relevant to Evangelicals—is evangelism. A criticism of today's Evangelicals is that they don't evangelize. Author Christine Wicker writes of Evangelical

Christians: "There's one thing they're not doing. They're not evangelizing, and nobody, not even Jesus, seems able to make them do it."[15]

The 2008 Pew Religious Landscape Survey asked its respondents how often they shared their faith with non-believers or people from other religious backgrounds. (If the respondent was religiously unaffiliated, the question was changed to ask how often they shared their views on God and religion with religious people.) Figure 5.7 plots how many respondents shared their faith on a regular basis, which, for the sake of this graph, means doing it at least monthly if not weekly. Over half, 52%, of Evangelicals report that they share their faith with others at least monthly, as do 55% of Black Protestants. Far fewer Catholics, Mainline Protestants, and Orthodox Christians regularly share their faith, with between 21 and 26% reporting that they do. Among other religious groups, Jehovah's Witnesses are the champion faith-sharers, with a full 84% of them sharing at least monthly. Conversely, relatively few Jews and Hindus—less than 20%—share their faith with others.

Another aspect of commitment to mission is financial giving. Presumably, people who give more money to their church, temple, synagogue, or mosque are, on average, more committed to their religion than those who give less. Unfortunately, this is a difficult subject to research because people are reticent to discuss their finances with others—even researchers. Perhaps the most meaningful measure of charitable donations is in terms of the percentage of one's income that is given to others. In other words, someone who gives 10% of their income can be seen as more committed than someone who gives 1%, even if they both give the same dollar amount. The Empty Tomb is a research organization that studies giving levels among Christian churches. They have calculated per-member giving as a percentage of income. For various Protestant denominations, they take the amount of money given to that denomination and divide it by the number of members in that denomination and the members' income. Figure 5.8 plots the results since 1968. As shown, giving

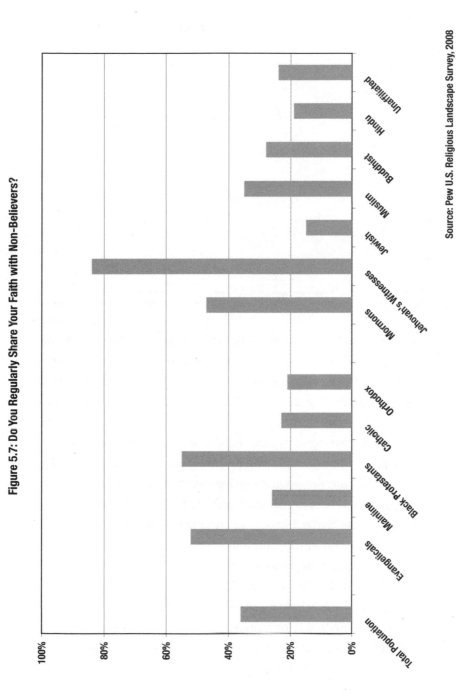

Figure 5.7: Do You Regularly Share Your Faith with Non-Believers?

Source: Pew U.S. Religious Landscape Survey, 2008

Figure 5.8: Protestant Giving Rates

Source: Empty Tomb Research

levels dropped from over 3% to about 2.5% through the mid-1980s, but they remained mostly stable over the subsequent twenty years.

Sociologists Christian Smith and Michael Emerson, in their book *Passing the Plate*, take an in-depth look at Christians' financial generosity.[16] Rather than starting with a fear message, they seek to motivate Christians to give more by describing the "almost unimaginable potential for good" if American Christians gave more generously. According to Smith and Emerson, generous giving would "transform the world"— bringing about massive and unprecedented social, cultural, and even spiritual change that reflects Christian values.[17] Given all the potential benefits of increased giving, the authors ask why Christians don't give more. Using data from various sources, they test numerous explanations, and they find the most evidence for the following: American Christians are unduly influenced by our society's consumerist culture; clergy do not boldly ask for money; Christians do not make their giving structured and routine; and Christians are suspicious of waste and abuse by the administrators of nonprofit organizations.[18]

Religious Experiences

Another facet of religion for Christians is with regard to experiences that aren't easily explained by day-to-day life. In other words, we consider them supernatural. My own exposure to supernatural experiences got off to a funny start. When I was in college, some friends got involved with a charismatic church, a Vineyard Christian Fellowship, and they invited me to come along to a healing meeting. At the prompting of the speaker, I put my hands out, turned my palms up, and invited God to fill me with his Holy Spirit. Soon after I did so, I felt a warm tingling on my left arm. The speaker hadn't mentioned this as something that commonly happens, but I thought it was a good sign that the whole thing worked as it was supposed to. I then noticed that if I moved the position of my arms, the tingling would increase or decrease in intensity. This, I figured, was some sort of object lesson about obedience that I would want to tell my friends about. This went on for about five minutes until I noticed that I was standing next to a heating vent that was shooting warm air up. Oops. (I've since had other supernatural experiences that were more difficult to explain away.)

Perhaps the most commonly referenced religious experience is having a sense of joy and peace; in fact, this experience is often used to promote the value of a religion to non-believers. A Pew Survey question asked respondents how often they "feel a deep sense of spiritual peace and well-being." About two-thirds of Evangelicals and Black Protestants report feeling these positive emotions on a weekly if not daily basis. In contrast, slightly less than half of Catholics, Mainline Protestants, and Orthodox Christians report them. Among other religious groups, about three-fourths of Mormons and Jehovah's Witnesses report spiritual peace and well-being while only about one-third of Jews and the religiously unaffiliated do.

Another supernatural outcome is healing. Here the survey question asks if the respondent has ever "experienced or witnessed a divine healing of an illness or an injury," and Figure 5.9 shows that there is

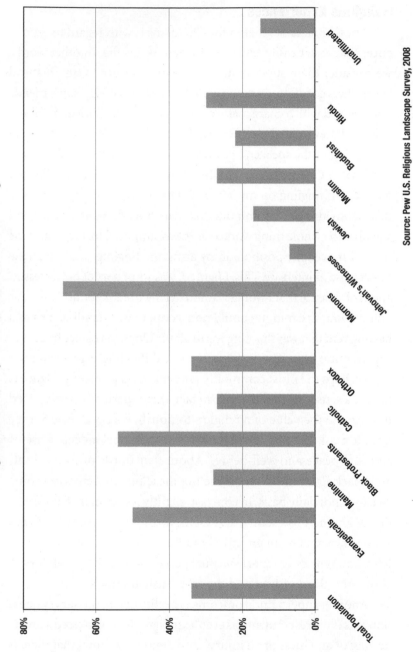

Figure 5.9: Have You Experienced or Witnessed a Divine Healing?

Source: Pew U.S. Religious Landscape Survey, 2008

a lot of variation in how members of different religions answer. Half or more of Evangelicals and Black Protestants report having experienced such a healing, whereas only about a quarter of Catholics and Mainline Protestants have. A full 69% of Mormons report healings, compared to only 15% of Jews and 7% of Jehovah's Witnesses.

We're Losing the Young, Part II

The general fear of a watered-down Christianity is even more pronounced when Christians talk about young people. Josh McDowell, for example, laments that "the obvious shocking truth is that we are not seeing the majority of churched youth transformed by the power of God."[19] The problem is so bad, according to McDowell, that the church faces "a generation of young people who no longer hold to what most evangelicals consider to be the true foundations of the Christian faith."[20] To highlight this fear even more (and to make it more believable by using statistics), McDowell cites a study attributed to The Barna Group: "Research showed that 98% of professed born-again young people do 'believe in Christ,' *but they do not reflect Christlike attitudes or actions.*"[21] The fear message here is that even if young people stay in the church, they certainly are not acting like good Christians, at least not compared to how young people used to be. There's an element of cranky nostalgia here. Kids today are no good, not compared to how it was in the old days. The question that I pose is whether there's any evidence that supports this type of nostalgia.

It's reasonably straightforward to test this claim; we simply need to compare today's Christian young people with those of the past, and Figure 5.10 does this with Christian beliefs. Using data from the General Social Survey, it plots how many young Evangelicals (defined as ages eighteen to twenty-nine) are certain in their belief in God, have a literal interpretation of the Bible, believe in life after death, and view themselves as strong Evangelicals.

What may surprise many if not most Christians is that the

beliefs of young Evangelicals over the past several decades have either remained stable or have become more in line with the church's teachings. In the late 1980s, about 75% of young Evangelicals were certain in their belief in God. Now the number has increased slightly, approaching 80%. Back then, about 55% of young Evangelicals believed that the Bible is the literal Word of God (as opposed to the inspired Word or simply a book of fables). This number has stayed about the same over time. In the 1970s, about 80% of young Evangelicals believed in life after death. Now the percentage is getting closer to 90%. Finally, in the 1970s, only about one-third of young Evangelicals viewed themselves as "strong evangelicals." Now the number is about 50%.

Figure 5.10: Beliefs of Young Evangelicals

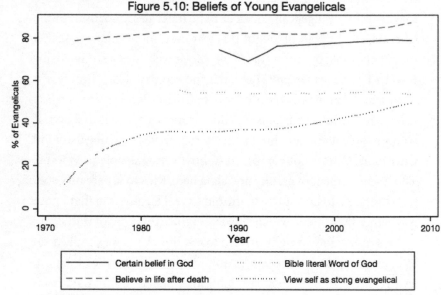

Source : General Social Survey

But once again we must ask the question of whether beliefs translate into actions. Let's look at religious activities, including prayer, church attendance, and evangelism. As shown in Figure 5.11, the percentage of young Evangelicals who pray daily has steadily increased, from about half in the 1980s to over two-thirds currently. Church attendance has likewise trended upward, with about 35% of evangelical youth attending church weekly in the 1970s and 1980s and over 40% now. The data for sharing their faith is based on only three data points, so conclusions are tentative, but it appears that the number of young Evangelicals who share their faith has remained steady if not increased since the late 1980s.

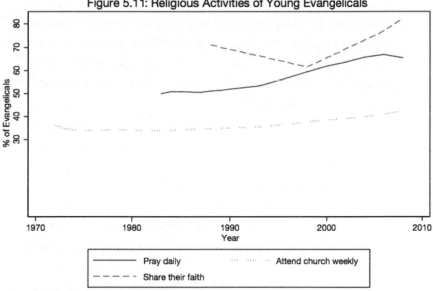

Figure 5.11: Religious Activities of Young Evangelicals

Source : General Social Survey

While it's entirely natural for us old folks to worry about the young, there isn't a lot of evidence to back up our fears. If anything, today's evangelical youth are even more committed to their Christian beliefs and more active in expressing their faith than we were back in the day. Not only that, but today's youth don't wear the ugly disco clothes and wacky hairstyles of the 1970s.

Does Church Attendance Make a Difference? Some Thoughts About Barna's *Revolution*

In the context of talking about Evangelicals' beliefs and practices, let's turn to an argument made by George Barna in his 2005 book, *Revolution.* In it he identifies a "new breed of disciple of Jesus Christ."[22] Termed "Revolutionaries," these new Christians aren't interested in merely playing church. Instead, they want to aggressively advance God's kingdom. They are like super-spiritual, Christian commandos. They are "constantly worshiping and interacting with God." They demonstrate "complete dedication to being thoroughly Christian by viewing every moment of life through a spiritual lens and making every decision in light of biblical principles." They are "determined to glorify God every day through every thought, word, and deed in their lives."[23] According to Barna, there are about 20 million of these super-Christians.[24]

A key feature of Revolutionaries, Barna tells us, is their ambivalence toward church. For Revolutionaries, there is nothing wrong, per se, with most churches, but they have no interest in playing "religious games." He claims that the church is somewhat tangential in the formation of Revolutionaries, and so they are not involved in churches any more than non-Revolutionaries are. He writes: "Our research indicates that Revolutionaries fill all points on the continuum of church involvement."

From Barna's perspective, if Christian churches did their job properly, people who attended church more often would live their lives more in line with biblical principles. In his own words:

> If the local church were the answer to our deep spiritual need, we would see two things. First, people who were most heavily involved in a Christian congregation would be more spiritually developed than others. Second, churched Christians would increasingly reflect the principles and characteristics Scripture tells us are the marks of Jesus' true disciples.[25]

Unfortunately, Barna concludes, Christian churches are not doing their job; hence the need to identify and cultivate Revolutionaries.

In statistical language, Barna claims that there is no correlation between church attendance and Christian beliefs and practices, and this is a simple claim to test. Previously in this chapter, I examined various Christian beliefs and activities, so let's see if they are more prevalent among the people who attend church more often.

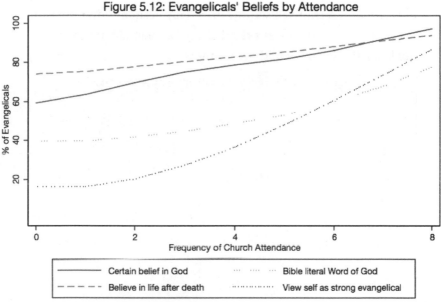

Figure 5.12: Evangelicals' Beliefs by Attendance

Source : General Social Survey 2000 - 2008

Figure 5.12 looks at the relationship between religious beliefs and church attendance among Evangelical Christians. The measure of church attendance goes from zero, never attending, to eight, attending several times a week. If Barna is correct, we would see horizontal lines across this figure, indicating that Christian beliefs do not vary with church attendance. What we see, however, is very different. Among the Evangelicals who never attend church, only 60% have a certain belief in God; in contrast, nearly all of the most frequent attendees do.

127

Likewise, only 40% of the less-frequent attendees believe in the Bible as the literal Word of God, whereas 80% of the most frequent attendees do. Seventy-five percent of the less-attendees believe in life after death, compared to 90% of the more frequent attendees, and only 20% or so of those who do not attend view themselves as strong Evangelicals, compared to 80% of those who attend most frequently.

We see a similar pattern with Christian activities. As shown in Figure 5.13, only about half of Evangelical Christians who never or rarely attend church also pray on a daily basis, but over 90% of the most regular attendees pray daily. An almost identical pattern holds for sharing one's faith with others.

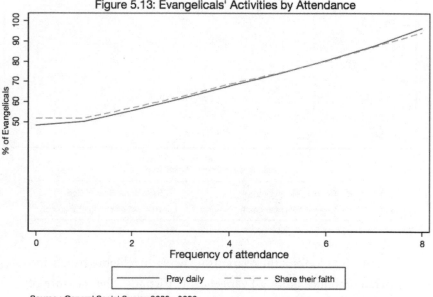

Figure 5.13: Evangelicals' Activities by Attendance

Source : General Social Survey 2000 - 2008

The strong relationship between church attendance and Christian practice is well-established. Sociologist Robert Wuthnow, also examining data from the General Social Survey, concludes that "the differences between regular church attendees and those who attend less regularly . . . are dramatic." Specifically, he found that regular attendees are more likely to look to God for strength, believe that God is watching over them, carry their religious beliefs into other dealings, feel God's presence every day, find comfort in religion, desire closeness to God, consider themselves to be very religious and spiritual, and have had a life-changing religious experience.[26]

From these analyses, it appears that Barna's *Revolution* has it wrong. Not just a little wrong, but a lot wrong. You will find the most devoted, most active Christians in church on Sunday mornings. That is not to say that there aren't fine Christians who do not attend church, but the best Christians usually do, and they do so regularly.

CHAPTER 6

Have Christians Gone Wild?

Conventional religion is not an effective force for moral behavior or against criminal activity.

—*Bernard Spilka, Ralph Hood, and Richard Gorsuch, Psychologists*

Scandalous behavior is rapidly destroying American Christianity.

—*Ron Sider, Professor, Eastern Theological Seminary*

Evangelical Christians are as likely to embrace lifestyles as hedonistic, materialist, self-centered, and sexually immoral as the world in general.

—*Michael Horton, Theologian*

Several years ago, I started a blog about Christianity and sociology (*www.brewright.blogspot*), and one of the first issues I examined was Christian divorce rates. For years I had heard that Christians had divorce rates higher than anyone else, but this didn't make sense to me because I know how much churches value and encourage marriage.

In fact, I don't know if my own marriage would have survived its early years without the considerable support that we received from our church. I examined data from several sources, and I found that much of the prevailing wisdom on the matter was wrong. I posted my findings in a thirteen-part series on the topic,[1] and it stirred a lot of interest. I received many e-mails that expressed appreciation that someone was taking an in-depth, careful look at this issue. (I also got an e-mail asking for marital advice . . . um-m-m-m, don't have much to offer there.) This whole process got me interested in testing the conventional wisdom about American Christianity, and one thing led to another, and now I'm writing this book.

The general focus of this chapter is to examine how many Christians are doing activities that go against Christian principles. Certainly there are a lot of different activities that I could examine, but I will focus on issues of marriage, sex, crime, substance abuse, and everyday dishonesty.

Marriage Status

Christianity advocates that long-term sexual partnerships occur in the context of marriage, and once people are married, they should stay married. This is not to imply that divorce is always wrong—one can easily imagine situations where a pastor might counsel divorce, such as with an abusive spouse. However, all else being equal, staying married is preferred.

The General Social Survey asks questions about cohabitation (living with a romantic partner outside of marriage) and divorce rates. Christians, Jews, and members of other religions all have relatively low rates of cohabitation, around 4%. In contrast, twice as many of the religiously unaffiliated, over 8%, are living together. Among Christians, Mainline Protestants and Evangelicals have the lowest cohabitation rates.

As for divorce, the survey reports how many respondents (who had ever been married) had been divorced or were currently separated from their spouse. Contrary to popular belief, Christians and members of other religions have lower divorce rates, about 42%, than do the religiously unaffiliated, about 50%. Among Christians, however, there was substantial variation. Catholics are the least likely to have divorced, at 35%, followed by Mainline Protestants (41%), Evangelicals (46%), and Black Protestants (54%).

But if we want to know whether or not the evangelical church's teachings affect the actions of its members, perhaps an even more important question is whether cohabitation and divorce rates go down as church attendance goes up. As it turns out, they do, and the change is substantial. As shown in Figure 6.1, of the Evangelicals who rarely if ever attend church, 7% were cohabitating, compared to 5% of the monthly attendees and only 2% of the weekly attendees. Likewise, with divorce, 60% of the never-attendees had been divorced or were separated compared to only 38% of the weekly attendees.

These statistics are surprising, not because they are counterintuitive but because we've been told for so long that when it comes to marriage, Evangelical Christians are no different than non-Christians. Why is this myth so popular? Let me tell you a story about people's reactions to statistics about Christianity. I periodically read Digg.com, which is a user-driven news Web site. Readers nominate news stories and then vote for those that interest them the most. All stories start out the same, but those that get more votes, or "diggs," are featured more prominently on the Web site, and more people read them. In May 2007, I read a just-posted story entitled "Atheist divorce rate is lower than Christian" based on a study by George Barna. Since I had what I thought were more accurate data, similar to those presented above, I posted a second story with a parallel—but reversed—title: "Christian divorce rates are lower than atheist." I kept the format and length of the story about the same.

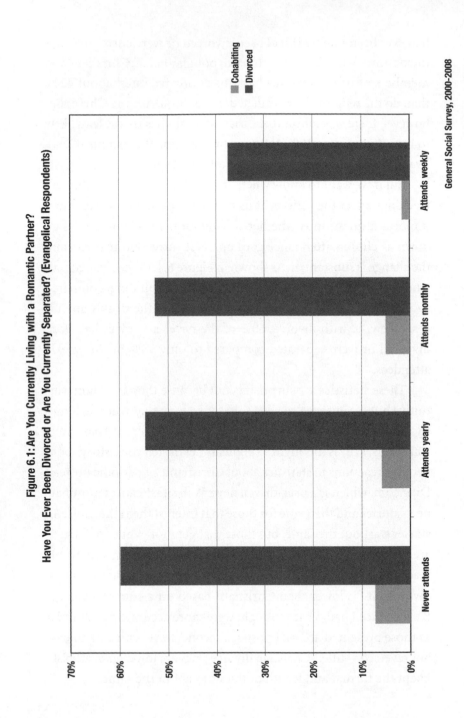

Figure 6.1: Are You Currently Living with a Romantic Partner?
Have You Ever Been Divorced or Are You Currently Separated? (Evangelical Respondents)

General Social Survey, 2000-2008

As a result, that morning there were two stories on Digg. com about Christians and divorce rates. Which received the most reader interest? It wasn't even close. The story portraying Christians negatively, i.e., with *higher* divorce rates, received over 3,500 "diggs," making it one of the top stories of the thousand or so submitted that week. The story portraying Christians positively, i.e., with *lower* Christian divorce rates, received less than a dozen "diggs."[2]

This illustrates a larger point. Negative statistics about Christianity receive more attention than positive ones, and consequently are more likely to become conventional wisdom. There are various possible explanations for this, as discussed in chapter 1. But in general, Christians acting like Christians just isn't as interesting as "Christians gone wild." As a result, bad news about Christians spreads faster and farther than good news.

Getting back to divorce statistics, even though Christians, especially those who regularly attend church, are doing relatively well in this area, there is some bad news. Cohabitation and divorce rates in recent decades have increased substantially for all groups, including Evangelicals. Since the 1970s, cohabitation rates among Evangelicals have increased from below 1% to almost 4%. Similarly, the percentage of divorced or separated Evangelicals almost doubled from the 1970s to the 2000s (25 to 46%).[3]

Domestic Violence

There are many other aspects of marriage that we can examine, but I want to focus briefly on a particularly disturbing problem—domestic violence. The analysis presented here comes from a unique data set—the National Survey of Families and Households. This study interviewed several thousand respondents as well as their romantic partners. The data were collected in the late 1980s, which makes them older than I would prefer, but their uniqueness makes them worth examining. Rather than reanalyzing the data myself, I am reprinting findings from a study by sociologist Christopher Ellison and colleagues.[4]

The National Survey of Families and Households asked married and cohabitating respondents whether they had hit, shoved, or thrown something at their partner in the previous year. In analyzing these data, Ellison and his colleagues classified Protestants as either "conservative," "moderate," or "liberal" based on their denominational affiliation. About 3.5 to 5% of Protestant and Catholic respondents reported committing domestic violence. This was less than the 6 to 8% of the religiously unaffiliated, but the differences between these groups weren't meaningful (i.e., statistically significant).

The big difference, however, came with church attendance. As shown in Figure 6.2, among Christian respondents almost 6% of the men who rarely attended church reported hitting, shoving, or throwing something at their partner in the previous year, compared to only 2% of the weekly attending men. Women displayed a similar pattern. Almost 8% of the never-attendees had hit, shoved, or thrown something at their partners, as compared to just over 3% for weekly attendees.

Here is where the uniqueness of the National Families and Households Study comes into play. Because it collects data from romantic partners, it allows us to compare self-reports of domestic abuse with partner-reports, and they mostly agreed. For example, men who frequently attended church reported committing less domestic violence, and their partners agreed with them. Likewise, women frequent-attendees reported committing less violence, and their partners agreed. In other words, partner reports produce the same pattern of findings as self reports presented in Figure 6.2, so we can feel more confident in the report's accuracy.

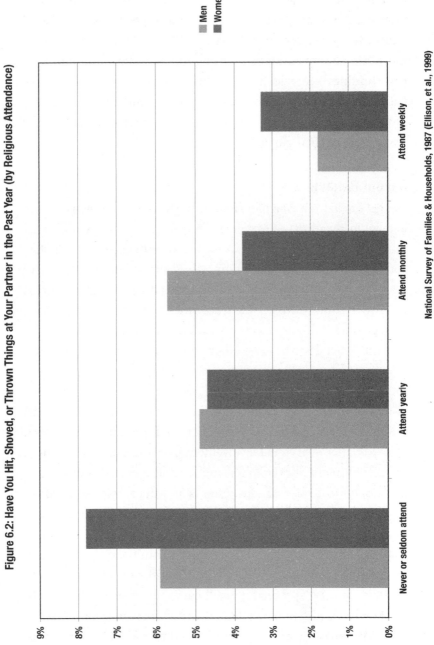

Figure 6.2: Have You Hit, Shoved, or Thrown Things at Your Partner in the Past Year (by Religious Attendance)

National Survey of Families & Households, 1987 (Ellison, et al., 1999)

This finding addresses a nagging methodological issue when studying Christians' misdeeds. If Christians report fewer misdeeds than others, are they actually behaving differently or are they simply more reluctant to admit their wrongdoings?[5] These domestic violence findings offer evidence that Christians—as well as others—are telling the truth, because the partner reports parallel the respondent reports. If they were lying, we'd expect their own reports to differ from those of their partners.

Sexual Behavior

Let's turn to an even more interesting topic—sex. When it comes to religion, the media, in particular, loves stories about sex and sexual misconduct. In looking at the sexual behavior of Christians, I'll start with extramarital sex. At this point, allow me to interject that there is a crucial distinction between extramarital sex and extra marital sex. One is committing adultery, the other represents a better-than-average week, and they have very different consequences.

The General Social Survey asks respondents if, when married, they have ever had sex with someone other than their husband or wife. As shown in Figure 6.3, 16% of Evangelicals reported that they had committed adultery at some time in their life. (It's worth noting that the way the question is worded, we don't know if the adultery happened before or after their initial involvement in evangelical Christianity). Mainline Protestants, Catholics, and Jews all reported similarly low levels of 14 to 16%. Black Protestants and the religiously unaffiliated reported the highest rates of extramarital sex, at about 25%. If we focus on the line labeled "Christians (all)" we see that, taken as a whole, Christians are committing adultery about one-third less than the unaffiliated. It appears that the commandment "Thou shalt not commit adultery" is, thankfully, still having an effect on the church.

Figure 6.3 also presents two other measures of sexual misconduct—promiscuity and viewing X-rated movies. The measure of

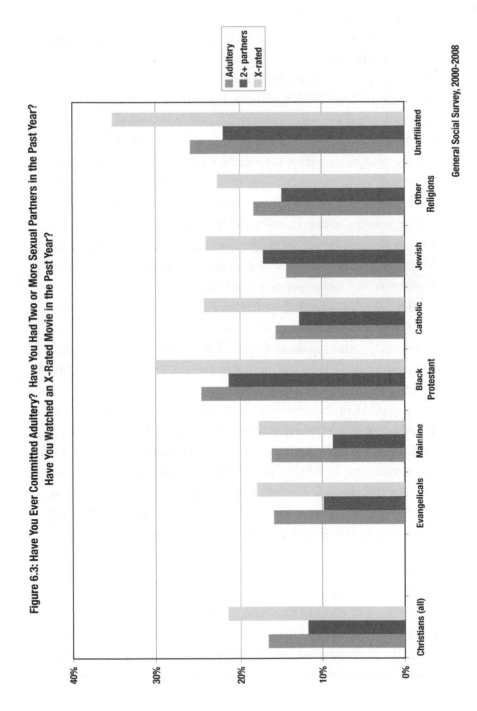

Figure 6.3: Have You Ever Committed Adultery? Have You Had Two or More Sexual Partners in the Past Year? Have You Watched an X-Rated Movie in the Past Year?

General Social Survey, 2000-2008

promiscuity asks if respondents have had two or more sexual partners in the previous year.[6] Evangelicals and Mainline Protestants had the lowest percentage of respondents reporting promiscuity, 8 to 9%, compared to 12% of Catholics, 17% of Jews, and 21% of Black Protestants and the religiously unaffiliated. With pornography, the question asks respondents if they have seen an X-rated movie in the previous year, and we see a similar pattern as that found with the adultery and promiscuity questions. At the low end, about 18% of the Evangelical and Mainline Protestant respondents reported having seen an X-rated movie, and at the high end 30% of Black Protestants and 35% of the religiously unaffiliated had. Again, if we look at "Christians (all)," we see a substantial difference between those who profess Christianity and the unaffiliated.

Just as we discovered with divorce rates, church attendance correlates well with sexual misconduct. As shown in Figure 6.4, Evangelicals who regularly attend church display far less sexual misconduct than those who attend less often. Twenty-two percent of Evangelicals who never attend church have committed adultery as compared to 13% of those who attend weekly. When it comes to promiscuity, 10% of Evangelicals who rarely attend church reported having had multiple partners, compared to 6% of weekly attendees. With pornography, 28% of those who rarely attended church had seen X-rated movies, compared to only 10% of those who attend weekly. Again, as was mentioned in the previous chapter, the best Christians tend to be those who go to church regularly.

Sex Among Our Youth

We pay a lot of attention to the sexual misbehavior of young people, and the prevailing belief is that our children are sexually active. To examine this question, I have analyzed data from the first wave of the National Study of Youth and Religion, collected in 2003, which gathered data from adolescents

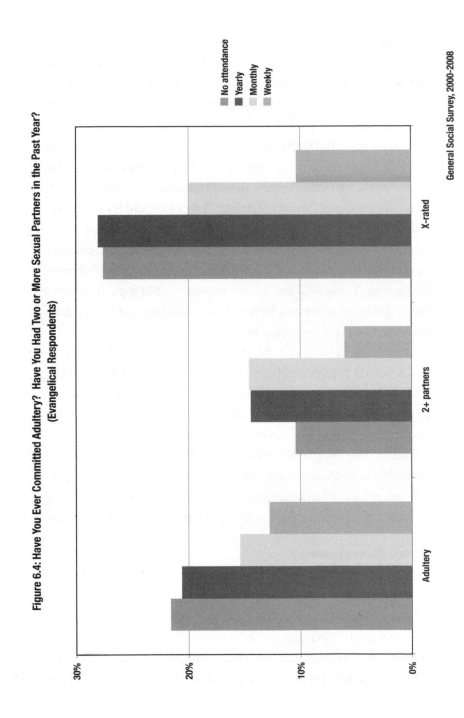

Figure 6.4: Have You Ever Committed Adultery? Have You Had Two or More Sexual Partners in the Past Year? (Evangelical Respondents)

General Social Survey, 2000-2008

ages thirteen to seventeen. According to this study, a little over 20% of conservative Protestant youth have had sexual intercourse and slightly more have had oral sex. This is lower than the religiously unaffiliated youth, of whom 30% had intercourse and 31% oral sex.

Sociologist Mark Regnerus, in his book *Forbidden Fruit: Sex and Religion in the Lives of American Teenagers*, describes what he refers to as a new middle-class morality about sex. This morality, especially prominent among Mainline Protestants and Jews (historically among the wealthiest religious groups), views vaginal sex as dangerous because of its potential for unwanted pregnancy, sexually-transmitted disease, and other problems that might diminish one's life choices. Those who live by this morality trade high-risk intercourse for other lower-risk forms of sex including oral sex, mutual masturbation, and pornography.[7]

In this social context, how can Christianity effectively promote sexual virtue? Regnerus points to the importance of teenagers being in a network of like-minded friends, family members, and authority figures. This network can teach religious values, and it also offers a place where these values can be reinforced.[8] Evidence for the effectiveness of this approach can be seen in the data. According to the National Study of Youth and Religion, there is a strong correlation between church attendance and sexual behavior. Both intercourse and oral sex decrease significantly with weekly church attendance.

Sex and Church Leadership

The analyses above look at the average Christian, but what really makes news is sexual misconduct by clergy. Jim Bakker, Jimmy Swaggart, Ted Haggard, and various Catholic priests have all received extensive media coverage for their sexual misdeeds. Recently *The Washington Post* published an article about sexual advances from clergy members to their congregants.[9] It was based on data from the

General Social Survey in which female respondents who attended religious services at least once a month were asked: "Since you turned eighteen, have you ever found yourself the object of sexual advances or propositions from a minister, priest, rabbi, or other clergyperson or religious leader who was not your spouse or significant other?" Based on the number of women who said yes, the article described sexual advances by clergy as a "problem so pervasive that it almost certainly involves a wide range of denominations, religious traditions, and leaders." It told the story of a worst-case scenario in which a pastor coerced a woman into sex in the context of giving her spiritual guidance, leading her to depression and an understandable distrust of the church.

Now, based on this description of the problem, you may be wondering just how many women have received this type of sexual attention from a clergy member. The answer is 3%. One in 33 churchgoing women reported that a religious leader had made a sexual advance to them. A friend who sent me this article asked a really good question: Is 3% a lot? It is certainly too much, since from a moral perspective even one case would be too much. But is it a lot? What standards can we use to interpret this number?

The General Social Survey suggests an answer, for it also asks the same respondents if they have ever been the object of sexual advances or propositions from their work supervisors. Obviously work supervisors are not a direct comparison to religious leaders. Not all women work, and those who do probably interact with their supervisors more than their pastors. Pastors and supervisors have different forms of authority, and their sexual misconduct can have very different consequences for the victim. Nonetheless, work supervisors probably constitute the closest comparison group to religious clergy. Whereas only 1 in 33 of the respondents reported clergy members making advances, a full 1 in 4 reported work supervisors doing so. These data suggest that women are much more likely to receive inappropriate sexual attention from authorities in the workplace than in a religious setting. Granted, the standards for clergy should be higher than those for work supervisors. But it is good to know that clergy appear to be doing much, much better in this regard than their secular counterparts.

Abortion

Before leaving the topic of sex, let's take a quick look at perhaps the most controversial of sex-related issues: abortion. Americans vary widely in their attitudes about the morality and legality of abortion, but rather than engage these issues, let's simply look at how many women of different religious faiths have had an abortion and whether that number decreases with church attendance. For this analysis I examine data from the National Survey of Family Growth, which interviewed thousands of women about all manner of reproductive issues. Catholic women were the least likely to have an abortion, with about 1 in 5 of them having done so. About 1 in 4 Protestant women have had abortions, and about 1 in 3 religiously unaffiliated women and members of other religions have had an abortion. Among both Protestants and Catholics, abortion rates dropped considerably with increased church attendance. About 1 in 3 Protestant women who rarely attended church had abortions compared to about half that rate, 1 in 6, of the weekly attendees. Likewise, among Catholic women, abortion rates drop from about 1 in 4 to about 1 in 8.

Crime

Turning our attention to crime, sociologists of religion have put forth various theories as to why religious affiliation should reduce criminal behavior. One popular explanation, offered by sociologists Travis Hirschi and Rodney Stark, points to the promises of supernatural punishments, in addition to those received here on

Earth, as a deterrent.[10] In other words, when Christians commit crime, we face two judges.

To examine crime, I use data from the third wave of the National Longitudinal Study of Adolescent Health. This data set was collected in 2002, and it surveyed over 15,000 young adults ages eighteen to twenty-five nationwide. The survey asks respondents a variety of questions about their experiences with crime and the criminal justice system, and I analyze four of them. The first question asks respondents if they have "ever been arrested or taken into custody by the police." The next three ask if, in the past twelve months, respondents have deliberately damaged someone else's property, stolen something worth more than $50, or hurt someone in a fight badly enough that they needed medical attention.

There is a similar pattern across each measure. Overall, Protestants were the least criminal of the respondents. For example, 9% of the Protestants had been arrested, which was less than the 11% of Catholics, 13% of other religions, and 15% of the religiously unaffiliated. The Protestant respondents were also the least likely to have damaged property or stolen goods. Along with Catholics, they were less likely than the religiously unaffiliated to have been in a fight that resulted in hurting someone.

Not only did Protestants commit less crime, but also the Protestants who attended church on a weekly basis did so far less than other Protestants. Figure 6.5 plots these differences, and the weekly attendees had crime levels that were about half as high as the other, less-frequently-attending Protestants. For example, 4% of the weekly attendees had been arrested, compared to 8% of the monthly attendees, 12% of the yearly attendees, and 15% of those who never attend. Among the three specific types of crime—damaging property, stealing more than $50, and hurting someone in a fight—there wasn't much difference between the monthly, yearly, and never-attending

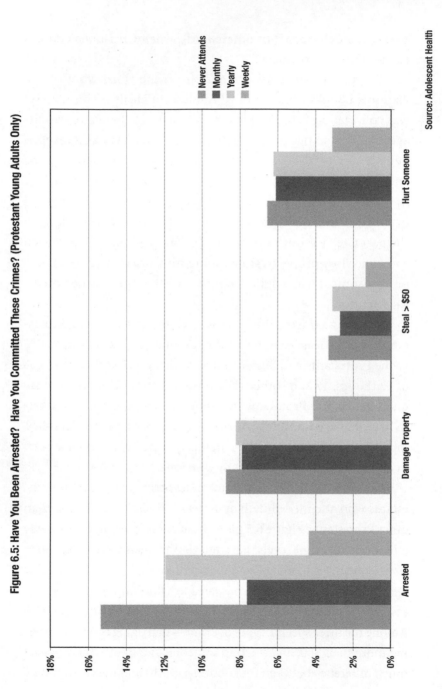

Figure 6.5: Have You Been Arrested? Have You Committed These Crimes? (Protestant Young Adults Only)

Source: Adolescent Health

groups, but all three of them had crime rates that were about double that of the weekly attendees.

Substance Abuse

Closely related to crime is the topic of substance abuse, and I'll examine three types: alcohol, marijuana, and other illegal drugs. Overall, I find that Christians in general, especially those who attend church, experience lower levels of substance abuse. The data for this section come from the 2002 National Comorbidity Study, a study of the physical and mental well-being of thousands of Americans.

The alcohol question that I looked at asks respondents if on the days that they drink, they typically have five drinks or more— a number chosen for its link with binge drinking. About 7% of Protestant respondents averaged five or more drinks when they drank, which was about the same as Catholics and members of other religions, but it was significantly lower—less than half—of the religiously unaffiliated. Fourteen percent of them reported five drinks or more. The marijuana question asks if respondents have used marijuana in the previous year. Just over 8% of Protestants had smoked marijuana, similar to Catholics (10%), but less than members of other religions (14%) and much less than the religiously unaffiliated (21%). With harder drugs, we see a similar pattern as with alcohol and marijuana. The question asks respondents if they had used illegal drugs such as cocaine, heroin, or LSD in the previous year. Two to 3% of Protestants, Catholics, and members of other religions had used these illegal drugs in the previous year, compared to nearly 6% of the religiously unaffiliated.[11]

Turning to attendance data, we see very large differences. Among Protestants, about 10 to 12% of the monthly, yearly, or rarely attending respondents averaged five drinks or more on the days they drank. In contrast, only 3% of the weekly attendees did. With marijuana, only 3% of the weekly attendees had smoked in the previous year,

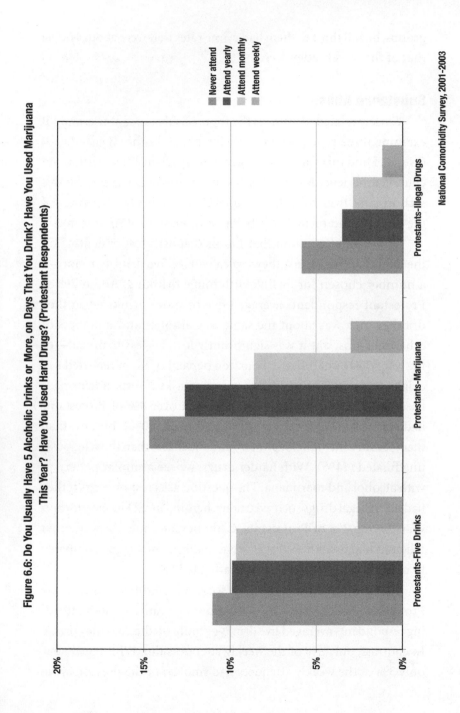

Figure 6.6: Do You Usually Have 5 Alcoholic Drinks or More, on Days That You Drink? Have You Used Marijuana This Year? Have You Used Hard Drugs? (Protestant Respondents)

National Comorbidity Survey, 2001-2003

Never attend
Attend yearly
Attend monthly
Attend weekly

compared to 9% of the monthly attendees, 11% of the yearly, and 15% of those who rarely attend. A similar pattern is seen with hard drugs. Six percent of Protestants who rarely attend church had used illegal drugs in the previous year, but this drops to 1% for the weekly attendees.

You've probably started to detect several patterns so far in this chapter. Christians are in fact more likely to follow Christian teachings about sexuality and morality than the religiously unaffiliated. The Bible makes certain statements about proper conduct for Christians, both for the sake of society as a whole as well as for personal health and wellness. Christians are certainly not perfect in following what the Bible teaches (in fact, one of the strongest claims that the Good Book makes is that no one is perfect), but the differences between Christian actions and those of the unaffiliated are not insubstantial. And what's more, the more committed Christians are to their faith, as measured by attending services, the more likely they are to "practice what they preach."

What does all this mean? Well, the white powder on the church pew is probably just baby formula. Also, this appears to be an area in which Christians are aware of and adhering to the church's teaching on morality. As discussed in chapter 1, this book makes no attempt to *explain* differences among religious groups—it simply tries to accurately report the differences. However, one interpretation of these findings is that the church has influence when it comes to changing behavior.[12]

Let's keep exploring this topic of morality with some questions that fall a little more into the gray areas of life.

Everyday Honesty

So far in this chapter, I've analyzed big wrongs—actions that many people in society disapprove of. But what about the smaller expressions of morality—those that occur in everyday life?

Sociologists have speculated that religion matters even more with everyday morality than it does with crime.[13] Various social institutions, such as the criminal justice system, exist to enforce criminal laws; in contrast, very few support everyday honesty, and so this is an area in which religious teachings can have an especially significant impact.

I actually had trouble finding suitable measures of everyday honesty, though I did find three in the General Social Survey that roughly fit into this concept. The first measure was collected in 1998, and it uses what sociologists call a "vignette question." This kind of question describes a hypothetical situation, and then asks respondents how they think they would respond in the situation. In this vignette, respondents are told to imagine that they are riding in a car driven by a close friend. The friend is speeding and hits a pedestrian, and then asks you to tell the police that he was in fact obeying the speed limit. Would you lie for your friend?[14] The second measure, collected in 2004, asks respondents if it's very important for American citizens *not* to evade paying their taxes. While this question measures *attitudes* about paying taxes rather than actual payment, we can assume reasonably that there is some link between attitudes and behavior. The third measure, collected in 2002 and 2004, asks respondents if during the past year they had received too much change from a cashier and not returned the excess money.

Overall, Evangelicals scored low on dishonesty. Only 8% of Evangelicals and 6% of Mainline Protestants said that they would lie to the police for a friend, compared to 14 to 15% of Black Protestants, Catholics, and members of other religions. Meanwhile, 20% of the religiously unaffiliated predicted that they would lie. Similarly, Evangelicals and Mainline Protestants were the least likely (21% and 24% respectively) to agree that paying taxes wasn't "very important," compared to 30% of Black Protestants, 31% of members of other religions, and 39% of the religiously unaffiliated. Finally, 44% of

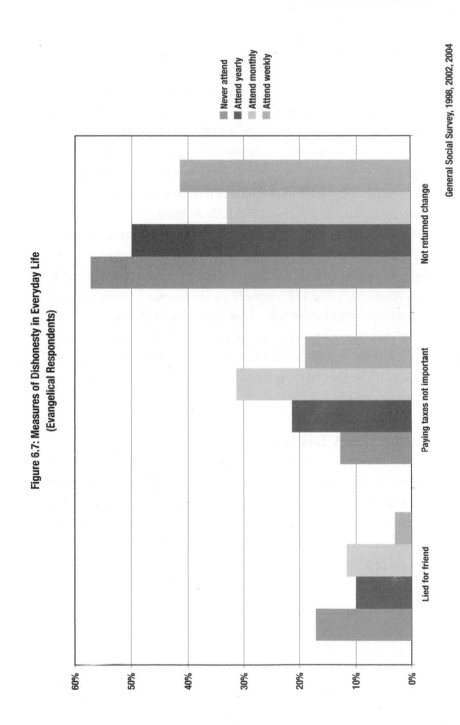

Figure 6.7: Measures of Dishonesty in Everyday Life
(Evangelical Respondents)

General Social Survey, 1998, 2002, 2004

- Never attend
- Attend yearly
- Attend monthly
- Attend weekly

Evangelicals reported that they had not returned excess change during the previous year, less than the 55% of religiously unaffiliated.

Turning to attendance measures, when it comes to everyday honesty the results are mixed for Evangelicals. A willingness to lie for a friend decreases considerably with church attendance. While 17% of the Evangelicals who rarely attend church would lie to the police, only 3% of the weekly attendees would do so. In contrast, there isn't a clear pattern between attitudes toward paying taxes and attendance. Nineteen percent of weekly attendees view paying taxes as not "very important," which is more than the never-attendees (13%) but less than the monthly attendees (31%). In regard to not returning excess change, the monthly and weekly attendees were the least likely (33% and 42% respectively) not to have returned excess change, compared to 57% of those who seldom attend.

It's not clear to me why those who attend church most frequently do not fare better in these measures; however, I would hesitate to read too much into this set of findings because the questions themselves are not a great fit for the concept that I am trying to measure.

So Where Does This Leave Us?

This chapter uncovers several general patterns regarding morality and religious affiliation. Essentially, people who associate themselves with Christianity, as compared to the religiously unaffiliated, are more likely to have faithful marriages, commit less crime, interact honestly with others, and not get into as much trouble with drugs or alcohol. What's more, the more committed Christians are to their faith, as measured by church attendance, the greater the impact the church's teachings seem to have on their lives.

Clearly from these analyses we know that Christians are not perfect. Many of the numbers may disappoint you or perhaps even shock you. But the question of what we should expect from Christians should be addressed. As I brought up in an earlier chapter, often those outside the church (and some inside the church) frequently accuse Christians of hypocrisy. But what does hypocrisy really mean? Is it simply doing something wrong that you know you shouldn't? If so, I don't know anyone, Christian or otherwise, who isn't a hypocrite. Everyone falls short of their own standards from time to time, whether they tell a lie when they know they shouldn't or drink one drink too many at a cocktail party.

But if we want to be precise with our definitions, that isn't hypocrisy. Hypocrisy is claiming to be something you're not. For instance, if you run for office proclaiming your unblemished record of honesty, but then are secretly taking bribes on the side, you're a hypocrite. If, on the other hand, you believe that lying is wrong but sometimes do it anyway, you're not. You're just human.

And, for better or worse, Christians are certainly human. Many of us lie, cheat, get drunk, etc., just like all the other billions of people on the planet. To some extent this is disappointing (because we should know better), but at the same time it shouldn't be unexpected (because we know ourselves). Granted, there are certainly some Christian hypocrites out there, but most of us just fall into the general category of "sinners."

As I mentioned in the introductory chapter, becoming a Christian doesn't make people good, it just makes them better. In other words, Christians believe that the Christian faith should, in fact, change how people live their lives, but this change isn't necessarily instantaneous. Rome wasn't built in a day, and it might take even longer to perfect a person than to build an empire. Our expectations, therefore, should not be that Christians are blemish-free, but rather that they are different than non-Christians when it comes to various measures of morality—specifically those "rights and wrongs" that the Bible and churches teach about. And, lo and behold, the research seems to bear this out.

To some extent this is a "dog bites man" story. In other words, when things occur the way we would expect them to, it's usually not newsworthy. But in this case, what *should* be expected is, in fact, surprising. Why? Because the vast majority of reports we hear, both secular and Christian, have been claiming for years that Christians are no more moral—and often less so—than everyone else. Overturning conventional wisdom? Cool.

CHAPTER 7

Do Christians Love Others?

"Being Christian" is no longer defined by doing good deeds.
—*Tom Gilroy, Writer and director*

"Christianity" has essentially become a mechanism for allowing millions of people to replace being a decent human being with something else, an endorsed "spiritual" substitute.
—*Richard Beck, Professor, Christian psychologist*

We have just enough religion to make us hate but not enough religion to make us love one another.
—*Jonathan Swift*

The last chapter asked if Christians are doing what is morally wrong, and this chapter asks the reverse question: Are Christians doing what's morally right? This is a broad question, and Christians vary widely in their understanding of what Christians should be doing. For example, charismatic Christians emphasize the importance of spiritual gifts such as healing, prophecy, words of knowledge, and speaking in tongues. Health-and-wealth churches emphasize success in both one's personal life and career. Far more obscure, but still derived from a reading of the Bible, are snake-handling sects in the rural South whose worship services involve actually handling snakes as a sign of God's work. If you've never seen footage from a snake handling service, look it up on the Internet—it's fascinating. Me? I very much dislike snakes. It's not quite a phobia, but I don't want them anywhere nearby while I'm worshiping. My limit would be handling gummy worms.

Given the wide range of Christian practices, I've decided to focus on the central command of loving others. Even love is a very broad concept, encompassing a variety of beliefs, attitudes, feelings, and actions. To my knowledge, no large-scale survey has asked questions designed specifically to measure the breadth of Christian love, so I had to rummage around a number of surveys looking for pertinent items.

As you've probably figured out already, I'm no theologian, and so I am not claiming that these survey questions are an ideal representation of Christian love. Rather, they were the best I could find. I divided these questions into three topics: Do Christians interact with their neighbors? Do Christians act virtuously? Do Christians love members of other groups? Of course, there is a lot more to love than just these three topics, but it seems rather straightforward that they are aspects of Christian love.

Interactions With Neighbors

If we Christians are to love other people, this would imply, at the very least, that we interact with them. There are many, many data sets that measure social ties—this is something that sociologists like to study—but I want to focus on neighbors. The concept of "neighbor" in Scripture is much broader than simply the people living near us, but it certainly includes them. The 2006 Social Capital

Community Study asks respondents how often they talk or visit with their immediate neighbors. As shown in Figure 7.1, Protestant respondents were the mostly likely (53%) to interact at least once a week with their neighbors, followed by Catholics (50%), those with no religious affiliation (46%), and members of other religions (44%). Among Protestants, there is a modest positive association between church attendance and interacting with neighbors. Whereas 49% of Protestants who never attended church talked or visited with their neighbors weekly, 56% of the weekly attendees did so.

Do Christians Love Others?

In looking at love, let's start with Christians' attitudes toward others. Two survey questions from the General Social Survey pertain to selflessness. The first asks how often the respondents feel a selfless caring for others, and the second asks how often they accept others even when others do things they think are wrong. Figure 7.2 plots how many respondents report doing these two things on a daily basis. Black Protestants, especially, and Evangelical Christians score highest on these measures, with about 40% or more agreeing that they selflessly care for and accept others. In contrast, only about 25% of the religiously unaffiliated report doing so.

Among Evangelicals, those who attend church services most frequently report the most caring and acceptance. About one-third of the never-attendees selflessly care for others on a daily basis compared to 45% of the more regular attendees. Similarly, only 26% of the never-attendees regularly accept others when they are wrong, but 46% of the weekly attendees do so.

Another aspect of Christian love is caring for the disadvantaged and exploited. The General Social Survey asks two questions in this regard. The first asks respondents if they are described well by the statement: "I often have tender, concerned feelings for people less fortunate than me," and the second asks respondents if they agree

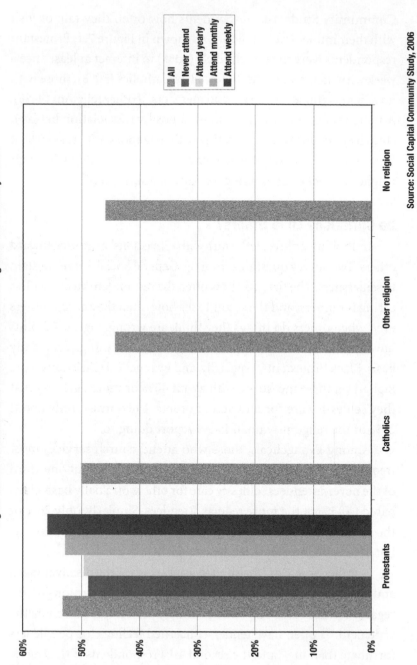

Figure 7.1: Do You Talk or Visit with Your Immediate Neighbors on a Weekly Basis?

Source: Social Capital Community Study, 2006

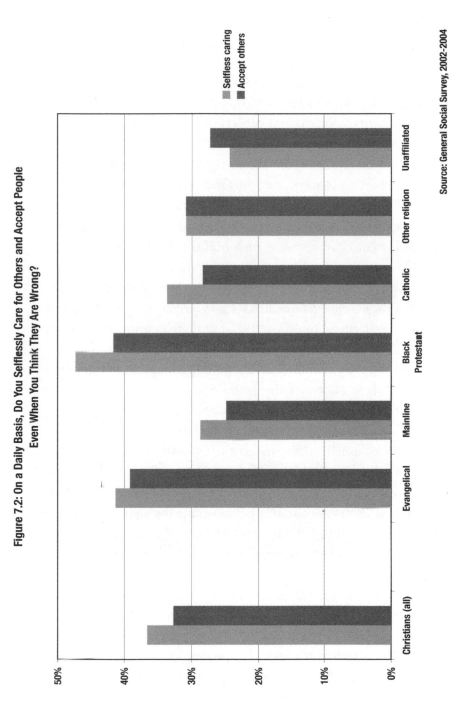

Figure 7.2: On a Daily Basis, Do You Selflessly Care for Others and Accept People Even When You Think They Are Wrong?

Source: General Social Survey, 2002-2004

with the statement: "When I see someone being taken advantage of, I feel kind of protective toward them." When it comes to how many respondents agree with these statements, Evangelicals score the highest on both measures. Eighty percent of the Evangelical respondents reported being concerned for those less fortunate, and 86% reported feeling protective toward those taken advantage of. In contrast, the religiously unaffiliated registered the lowest scores, with 68% reporting concern and 75% reporting feeling protective.

These empathetic feelings increase with church attendance among Evangelicals. Seventy-one percent of the Evangelical respondents who never attend church services are concerned about the less fortunate, which is significantly less than the 83% of the weekly attendees. When it comes to feeling protective of those who are taken advantage of, Evangelicals who attend church at least yearly score higher than those who never attend (85% vs. 81%), but there's curiously not much difference between those who attend yearly, monthly, or weekly.

Another attitude associated with Christian love is putting others' interests before our own. The General Social Survey has three relevant questions. They ask whether respondents agree with the following statements: "I would rather suffer myself than let the one I love suffer"; "I am usually willing to sacrifice my own wishes to let the one I love achieve his/hers"; and "I would endure all things for the sake of the one I love." Overall, three Christian groups—Evangelicals, Mainline Protestants, and Catholics—score the highest on all these measures, and Black Protestants and the unaffiliated scored lowest. The biggest difference occurred with the statement about "enduring all things." Eighty-five percent of Evangelicals somewhat or strongly agreed with this statement, along with 81% of Catholics; whereas about 71% of Black Protestants and members of other religions agreed with it, and only 66% of the religiously unaffiliated agreed.

One last relevant attitude is forgiving others. To be honest, this isn't one of my favorite commandments, for I would just as soon keep a close accounting of others' wrongs (while wanting my own wrongs forgiven, of course), but it is in the Book. The 1998 General Social Survey asked respondents if because of their religious and spiritual beliefs they always forgave those who hurt them. Overall, Protestant respondents—Evangelicals, Mainline Protestants, and Black Protestants—are the most forgiving, with 52 to 55% of them reporting that they always or almost always forgive others. About 45% of Catholics and members of other religions report always forgiving, and only 29% of the religiously unaffiliated do so.

Do Christian Actions Reveal Love?

So far I've focused on attitudes, but love expresses itself in actions as well—especially doing things for those in need. The General Social Survey asks two questions about involvement in charity: During the last twelve months, how often have you "given food or money to a homeless person" or "done volunteer work for a charity?" For simplicity, I identify how many respondents do it twice a year, figuring that anybody can do it once, but twice reflects more of a commitment. Forty-eight percent of Evangelical respondents had given food or money to the homeless twice or more in the previous year. This put them at the low end of the observed range, for 60% of the Black Protestants gave to the homeless as did slightly over half of Catholics and members of other religions. The Evangelical rate of giving is similar to the 44% of Mainline Protestants and religiously unaffiliated. With regard to volunteering for charities, Evangelical Christians did somewhat better. Mainline Protestants were the most likely to volunteer (43%), followed closely behind by Evangelicals (37%), members of other religions (35%), Catholics (33%), Black Protestants (31%), and, lastly, the religiously unaffiliated (25%).

The good news is that among Evangelicals, weekly attendees are the most likely to give to the homeless and volunteer for charities. As shown in Figure 7.3, 54% of Evangelicals who attend church every

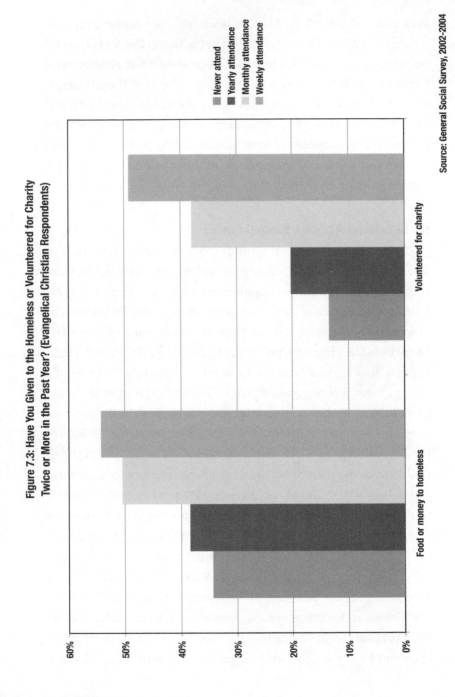

Figure 7.3: Have You Given to the Homeless or Volunteered for Charity Twice or More in the Past Year? (Evangelical Christian Respondents)

Source: General Social Survey, 2002-2004

week gave food or money to the homeless at least twice in the previous year, compared with only 34% of the never-attending ones. With charitable volunteering, the difference is even more pronounced. Forty-nine percent of weekly attendees volunteered compared to only 13% of the never attending.

Discussions of love often focus on large gestures, such as giving to the homeless or charities, but love also includes simple, everyday occurrences such as helping out friends or strangers. The General Social Survey asks several questions about everyday kindness: How often in the past year have you "looked after a person's plants, mail, or pets while they were away"; "offered your seat on a bus or in a public place to a stranger who was standing"; or "carried a stranger's belongings, like groceries, a suitcase, or shopping bag?" (Presumably this question about carrying a stranger's belongings refers to helping them, not stealing from them). According to the survey, there are some differences in people's answers associated with religion, but it varies by the measure. When it comes to looking after other people's stuff, Mainline Protestants and Evangelicals were the most likely to do so (52% and 46% respectively). But with offering a seat to others or helping them carry their stuff, on the other hand, Evangelicals and Mainline Protestants scored low. Members of other religions are the most likely to do both (35% and 40% respectively). These numbers may reflect differences in opportunities. For example, it's difficult to offer your seat to a stranger if you never take public transportation. ("Hey you, want to sit in my car?"), and so the variation to this question might reflect who is more likely to live in an urban setting as much as religious differences.

Among Evangelicals, those who rarely attend church were the least likely to do any of these everyday gestures. Those Evangelicals who attend church on at least a semi-regular basis were more likely to look after or carry people's stuff and/or to offer them a seat on the bus.

Attitudes Toward Other Social Groups

In this section, I return to love-related attitudes, and I focus on Christians' feelings toward people in various social groups, including those of a different social class, race, or sex.

How Do We Feel About the Rich and the Poor?

With social class, the Bible is abundantly clear about the need to assist the poor, and in fact, some religious traditions of Christianity have emphasized this as the primary message of the gospel.[1] Most Christians wouldn't take it that far, but there's no denying that the Bible emphasizes doing right by the poor. To paraphrase an old saying about the role of newspapers in society, the teachings of Christ lead us to comfort the afflicted and afflict the comfortable.

I had some difficulty finding a suitable measure of economic justice, because most of the survey questions on this topic focused on specific policies and interventions. For example, a question might ask if respondents thought the U.S. government should spend more money on programs for the poor. Unfortunately, questions like this conflate a concern for the poor with attitudes toward government involvement in social programs. Finally, I settled on two rather general questions drawn from the 2006 Social Capital Community Study. They use a "feeling thermometer" that asks respondents to rate how they feel about a group from 1 to 100 (the higher the number the more favorable you feel toward it). Presumably, those people most concerned about the plight of the poor would have the warmest feelings toward them.

Figure 7.4 describes respondents' feelings toward the poor as compared to the rich. As you can see, each of the four religious groups stated warmer feelings toward the poor than the rich, with Protestants and Catholics reporting the strongest preference for both the poor and the rich. In terms of the gap between poor and rich ratings, there wasn't a lot of difference between groups. Protestants, for example, rated the poor at 71 and the rich at 60, making for an

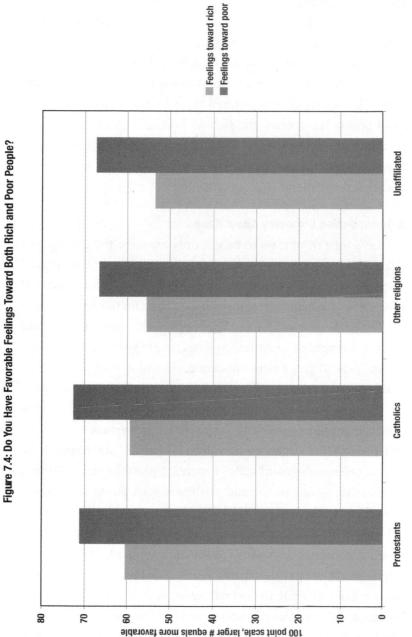

Figure 7.4: Do You Have Favorable Feelings Toward Both Rich and Poor People?

■ Feelings toward rich
■ Feelings toward poor

Source: Social Capital Community Survey, 2006

eleven-point difference. Members of other religions also had an eleven-point difference, and Catholics and the religiously unaffiliated had a thirteen-point difference.

Among Protestants, those who attended church services most frequently had the warmest feelings toward both the rich and the poor. The weekly attendees rated their feelings toward the poor at 74 points and toward the rich 63 points; whereas, those who rarely attended rated them at 66 and 55 points respectively. The gap between the rich and the poor remained steady, at 10 or 11 points, at each level of attendance.

A Disappointing Discovery About Race

Let's turn from class to race. I only examine the attitudes of Whites in this category, even though race-related attitudes of racial minorities are equally interesting. But unfortunately, the data that I'm using do not have enough minority respondents for this type of analysis. The analyses that I present here constitute, in my opinion, bad news for Evangelical Christians, so I'm going to go into greater depth on this issue to give a richer understanding of it; specifically, I will look at three separate survey questions regarding racial attitudes.

The first question is a type of feeling thermometer. The General Social Survey asks respondents "In general, how warm or cool do you feel toward Whites, Blacks, Asians, and Hispanics," and respondents answer on an eight-point scale.[2] Figure 7.5 plots the feelings of five different religious groups, and as shown, each group felt warmer toward Whites than toward Blacks, Asians, or Hispanics. In this sense, White Americans of any religious tradition as well as the religiously unaffiliated have plenty of room for improvement. There is some variation in feelings toward minorities, however, with members of other religions having the overall warmest feelings toward Blacks, Asians, and Hispanics. Catholics and the religiously unaffiliated had mid-range feelings toward racial minority groups, and the two

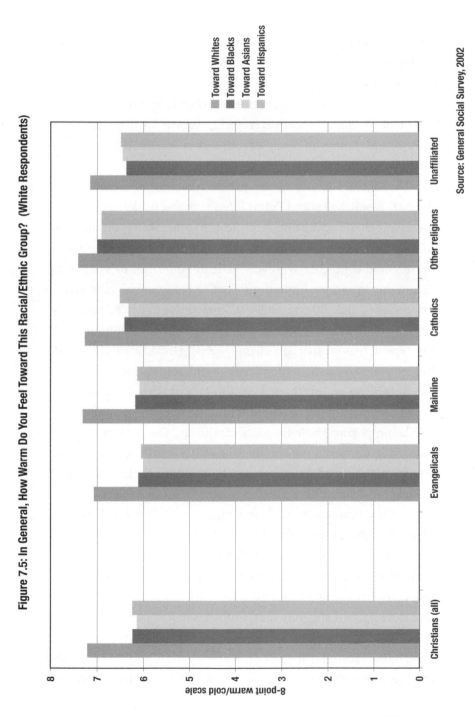

Figure 7.5: In General, How Warm Do You Feel Toward This Racial/Ethnic Group? (White Respondents)

Toward Whites
Toward Blacks
Toward Asians
Toward Hispanics

Source: General Social Survey, 2002

8-point warm/cold scale

Unaffiliated
Other religions
Catholics
Mainline
Evangelicals
Christians (all)

Protestant groups, Evangelicals and Mainline Protestants, had the coolest feelings toward racial minorities.

On a positive note, Evangelicals who attend church more often have warmer feelings toward minority groups than those who attend less often. Weekly attendees averaged ratings of 6.4 to 6.6 for these groups, and those who rarely attended or only attended yearly had ratings of 5.3 to 5.5.

The next race-related survey question that I examine comes from the 2007 Pew Religion and Public Life Study, and it asks respondents if they anticipate acting differently toward others solely on the basis of race. Specifically, would respondents be less likely to support a presidential candidate who was African-American or Hispanic? Again, due to sample limitations I am limited to analyzing White respondents; and unfortunately, too many respondents, especially Christians, answered yes to this question. As shown in Figure 7.6, this type of bias is especially strong against Hispanic candidates. A full 19% of Protestant respondents would hold a Hispanic candidate's ethnicity against them, as would 11% of Catholics and about 9% of members of other religions and the religiously unaffiliated. Similar proportions hold for Black candidates, albeit at substantially reduced levels. Seven percent of Protestants would be less likely to vote for a Black candidate, compared to 6% of Catholics and 3% of the religiously unaffiliated and members of other religions.

Among Protestants, with this question there is no clear relationship to church attendance. Those Protestants who rarely attend church and those who attend weekly were the most likely not to support a Hispanic candidate, and those who rarely attend or only attend on a yearly basis were the least likely for Black candidates. The absence of a clear pattern suggests that, unfortunately, this form of racial intolerance does not steadily diminish with church attendance.

The last race-related question is a classic in sociological research, and it asks how respondents would feel about "Having a close relative

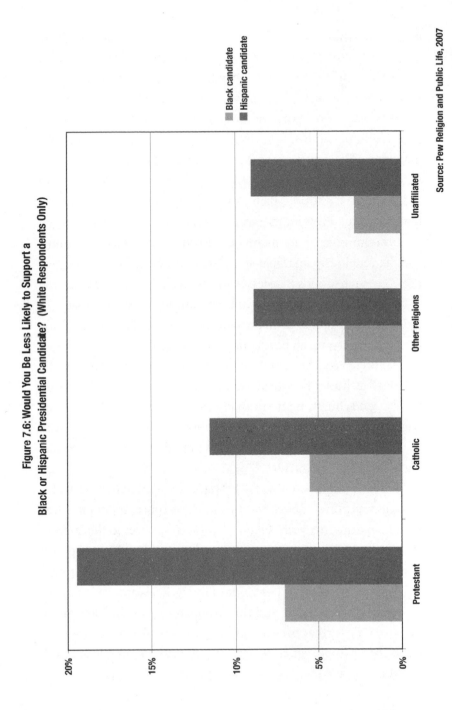

Figure 7.6: Would You Be Less Likely to Support a
Black or Hispanic Presidential Candidate? (White Respondents Only)

Black candidate
Hispanic candidate

Source: Pew Religion and Public Life, 2007

or family member marry a ____ person," with the blank being filled in by Black, Asian-American, or Hispanic-American. Once again, I'm examining only White respondents due to sample-size limitations.[3] According to the survey, opposition to marrying a non-White person varies widely by religion, and, overall, Evangelicals were the most opposed to it. A full 43% of Evangelicals opposed a close relative marrying a Black person, and around 30% opposed marriages to an Asian or Hispanic person. Mainline Protestants and Jews had less prejudicial attitudes than Evangelicals, and Catholics had less than Mainline Protestants and Jews. The two groups who scored the best, however, were members of other, non-Jewish religions and the religiously unaffiliated. Relative to Evangelicals, these two non-Christian groups were less than half as likely to hold prejudicial attitudes regarding marriage. Still, even among these most-tolerant groups, almost 20% of them opposed marriages to Blacks—showing that as a society, we all have a long way to go.

Among Evangelicals, there is no consistent pattern in interracial marriage attitudes by attendance. For example, Evangelicals who never attend church are the most likely to oppose White/Black marriages, but monthly attendees most oppose White/Asian-American marriages. Again, we see no evidence of prejudicial attitudes decreasing with church attendance.

If there is any good news for Evangelicals, it's that our racial attitudes, as well as everyone else's, appear to have substantially improved over the past twenty years. Figure 7.7 plots responses to the oppose-marriage question over the past twenty years, and as shown, opposition to interracial marriage has dropped substantially for all groups, including Evangelicals. In 1990, 77% of Evangelicals opposed marriage to an African-American, and this dropped to 50% in 2000, and it dropped even further, to 34%, in 2008. Is there still room to improve? Plenty, but it appears that society in general, including Evangelical Christians, is making progress on an almost yearly basis.[4]

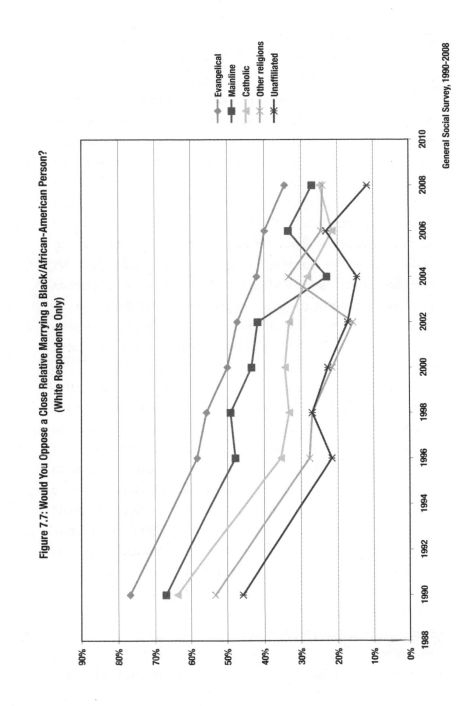

Figure 7.7: Would You Oppose a Close Relative Marrying a Black/African-American Person? (White Respondents Only)

General Social Survey, 1990-2008

Christians' Attitudes Toward Gays

The final set of attitudes that I want to consider are those toward gay people, and here things get a bit more complicated. Whereas no Christian would, or at least ever should, argue that being Black or Asian or Hispanic is a sin, Christians vary in their attitudes toward the sexual behavior of gay people. Some Christians view it as morally wrong, others do not. The wide range in attitudes toward gay sex is evidenced by a General Social Survey question that asked if "sexual relationships between two adults of the same sex [are] wrong," and the responses are plotted in Figure 7.8. As shown, about three out of four Evangelicals and Black Protestants think that gay sex is wrong, as do about half of Mainline Protestants and Catholics, a quarter of the religiously unaffiliated, and maybe 1 in 8 Jews. Furthermore, very few members of any religious group have uncertain attitudes toward gay sex, for the great majority of respondents view it as "always wrong" or "not wrong." In other words, there's not a lot of gray area for most people.

Reactions to homosexuality have sparked considerable controversy in the church, but regardless of attitudes toward the morality of gay sex, all Christians are called to love all people, and this would include gays. For some Christians, this falls under the heading of "loving the person but not their sin." So the question for us to explore is whether Christians have warm, charitable attitudes toward gay people. The answer, unfortunately, is no, and the same could be said for many non-Christians. The Social Capital Community Study asked respondents if they had favorable feelings toward gays and lesbians. Keep in mind that this question asked about attitudes toward gay people, not about their sexual behavior. The range was from 0 to 100, with 100 being the highest level of favorable feelings toward gay people. No group scored higher than 60 on this 100-point scale. The religiously unaffiliated and members of other religions averaged a score of 58, Catholics 54, and Protestants only 44 points.

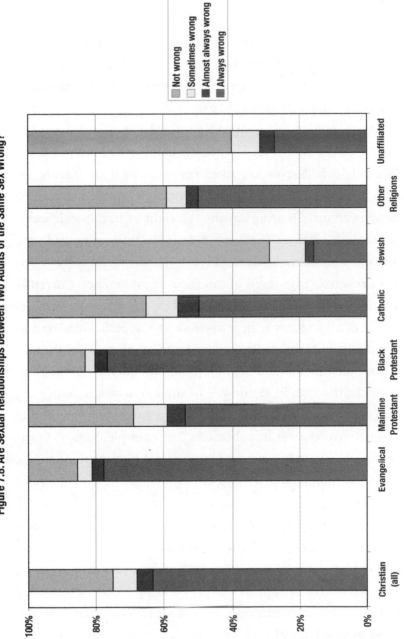

Figure 7.8: Are Sexual Relationships between Two Adults of the Same Sex Wrong?

Not wrong
Sometimes wrong
Almost always wrong
Always wrong

General Social Survey, 2000–2008

Furthermore, Protestants' feelings toward gay people do not become more favorable with church attendance. Weekly Protestant attendees have the most unfavorable feelings, scoring 40 points, but the next lowest group is those who never attend church, who score 46. In other words, there is not a clear, linear pattern between church attendance and feelings toward gays.

Another measure of attitudes toward gays is with regard to their involvement in everyday, public life. Since its inception, the General Social Survey has asked respondents if an "openly gay man wanted to make a speech in your community, should he be allowed to?" Denying anyone the right of free speech seems particularly harsh, and yet some people feel this way toward gays. As shown on the right side of Figure 7.9, Evangelical Christians show relatively high levels of this form of intolerance. Currently a little over one-quarter of Evangelicals and Black Protestants would disallow a gay man from making a speech, compared to about 12% of Mainline Protestants and Catholics, 8% of the religiously unaffiliated, and 5% of Jewish respondents. On the positive side, the lines in Figure 7.9 all slope downward, indicating that members of all groups have become increasingly accepting of gays' involvement in public life. For example, 52% of Evangelicals in the 1970s expressed disapproval of gays giving public speeches, compared to 45% in the 1980s, 30% in the 1990s, and 27% in the 2000s.

Yet again, Evangelicals' acceptance of others who are different does not increase with church attendance. Among Evangelical respondents surveyed since 2000, 28% of those who never or rarely attended church disapproved of gays making speeches, compared to 24% of the yearly attendees, 21% of the monthly attendees, and at the highest level, 31% of the weekly attendees.

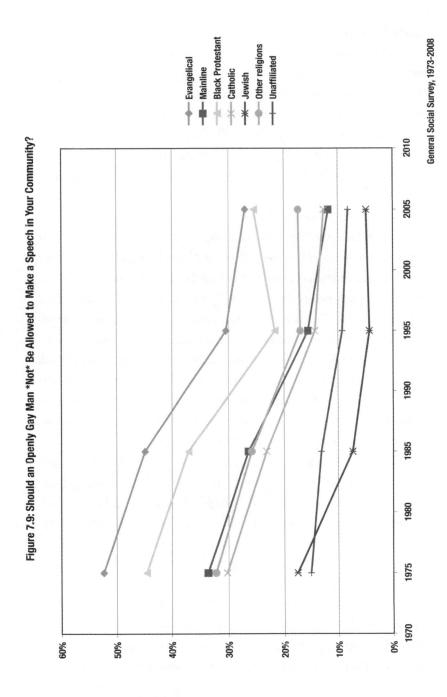

Figure 7.9: Should an Openly Gay Man *Not* Be Allowed to Make a Speech in Your Community?

General Social Survey, 1973–2008

Young People

So far this chapter has examined adults, but it's worth asking some of the same questions about young people. In particular, do Christian youth love others? Sometimes I wonder if we Christian adults focus so much on keeping our youth from doing wrong things, such as sex, drugs, and rock-n-roll, that we lose sight of whether they are doing right things, such as loving others.

The first analysis of Christian youth pertains to their relationships with their parents. The data here come from the National Study of Youth and Religion (Wave 2), a national study of high school-age kids.[5] The question asks the kids if they feel very close to their moms and dads. As it turns out, most of the kids feel close to their moms, and many feel close to their dads. Of the kids who affiliate with a religion, regardless of the religion, from 73 to 76% feel close to their moms. This is more than the 63% of the religiously unaffiliated children. A majority of Evangelical, Mainline, and Catholic kids (57%–58%) feel close to their dads compared to 52% of Black Protestants and 48% of the religiously unaffiliated. Among Evangelical high school kids, feelings of parental closeness increased with church attendance, especially with weekly attendance. (This is one more reason for me to take my kids to church!)

Turning to the behavior of Christian youth, the National Youth and Religion Study asked questions about volunteering, donating money, and helping needy people. As shown in Figure 7.10, Mainline Protestant youth were the most likely (43%) to do organized volunteer work on at least an occasional basis, followed by Evangelical youth (39%). Evangelical youth were the most likely (54%) to donate at least $20 of their own money to an agency or organization, followed by Mainline Protestant youth (46%). When it comes to directly helping neighbors, friends, or strangers in need, Black Protestants (51%) and members of other religions (48%) were the most likely to do so. Youth with no religious affiliation were the

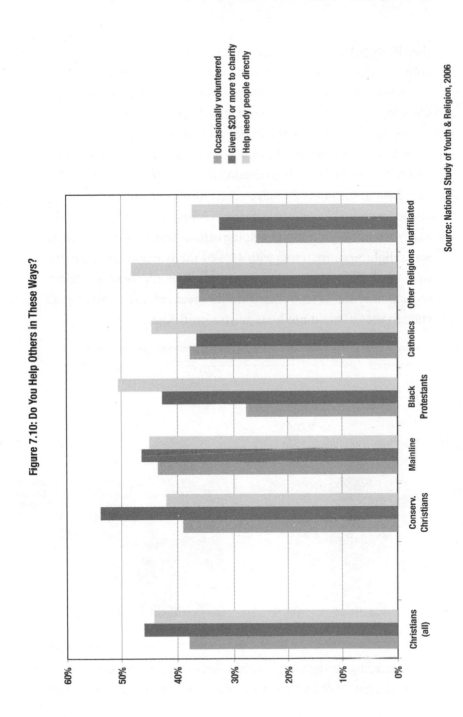

Figure 7.10: Do You Help Others in These Ways?

Source: National Study of Youth & Religion, 2006

least likely to be involved in all three charitable behaviors, whether volunteering, donating money, or directly helping others.

Among Evangelical youth, those who attended church more often were also the ones who were most likely to give their time and money to others. In fact, the weekly attendees were almost twice as likely to do these activities as the yearly attendees. Forty-five percent of the weekly attendees occasionally volunteered, compared to only 25% of the yearly attendees. Sixty-three percent of the weekly attendees gave $20 or more to charity, compared to only 35% of the yearly attendees. In terms of helping others directly, however, there was a slight negative trend, with 44% of the yearly attendees doing so but only 39% of the weekly attendees. It would be very difficult to guess why this is so, but statistically speaking, the trend is small enough that it might not have much significance.

Figure 7.11: Attitudes toward Blacks and Gays among White Evangelicals, by Age

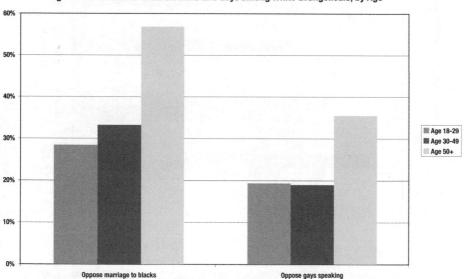

General Social Survey, 2000-2008

Regarding young people's attitudes toward members of other races and gay people, I return to the General Social Survey and reexamine two of the questions discussed above: Do respondents disapprove of a family member marrying a Black person, and do they oppose a gay man giving a public speech? Here I compare White Evangelical youth to middle-aged and older White Evangelicals, and as shown in Figure 7.11, young Evangelicals are the most tolerant and accepting of African-Americans and gays. Twenty-eight percent of the youngest White Evangelicals opposed interracial marriage, compared to a full 57% of the oldest Evangelicals. Nineteen percent of the young Evangelicals opposed a gay man giving a speech compared to 36% of the oldest respondents. As much as we older Evangelicals worry about our young people, maybe we have overlooked how we can learn from them.

Conclusion

Overall, this chapter is much more of a mixed bag than the others. With measures of love and compassion, Christians do very well as compared to the rest of society. They are neighborly, forgiving, and caring for the poor. And what's more, these measures of general goodwill toward others increase with church attendance, which suggests the possibility that churches effectively teach compassion.

On the other hand, when it comes to our feelings toward minorities, both racial and sexual, the news is not so good. Christians in general and Evangelicals in particular are the least accepting and favorably disposed toward those who are not like us. That said, our attitudes seem to be improving with time, and the young among us may be a bright spot as we look toward the future.

CHAPTER 8

What Do Non-Christians Think of Us?

Young people are quick to point out that they believe that *Christianity is no longer as Jesus intended.* It is UnChristian.
　　—*David Kinnaman and Gabe Lyons, UnChristian*

I probably wouldn't like Christians if I weren't one.
　　—*Dan Kimball, Christian author*

I am sorry that so often the biggest obstacle to God has been Christians.
　　—*Shane Claiborne, Esquire Magazine*

"Christianity has an image problem," warns the book *UnChristian*, written by Christian writers David Kinnaman, of The Barna Group, and Gabe Lyons. Examining data collected from several hundred young non-Christians, the authors conclude that, overall, non-Christians don't like Christians, especially Evangelicals. Kinnaman and Lyons find that about one-third of their sample had negative impressions of all Christians while one-half felt negatively toward Evangelical Christians. Only 3% had a good impression of Evangelicals. Underlying these negative attitudes, the non-Christian respondents viewed Christians as hypocritical, too evangelistic, anti-gay, sheltered, political, and judgmental.[1] Furthermore, the authors assert that young people's attitudes toward Christians have become increasingly negative over the past decade.[2] They write: "modern-day Christianity *no longer* seems Christian" [emphasis added].[3]

According to Kinnaman and Lyons, these negative perceptions limit the church's ability to fulfill its mission. If non-Christians do not like Christians, and they associate Christians with various negative beliefs and actions, then they will understandably be less interested in hearing the message of Christianity. As summarized in *UnChristian*, these negative attitudes "alter their willingness to commit their lives to Jesus."[4] George Barna elsewhere spells out the implications of *UnChristian* when he writes: "The public perception of our character and lifestyle is one of the major reasons why our evangelistic efforts in the United States have been so ineffective in the past quarter century."[5]

After defining these negative perceptions as a problem, Kinnaman and Lyons offer various guidelines for how Christians can act and present themselves differently to "address the unChristian perception of our faith." Among the authors' recommendations (all of which seem like good ideas): Act more like Jesus by connecting with people, being creative, serving people, and acting with compassion.

In this chapter, I want to examine the empirical claims made by *UnChristian* about the perceptions of Christians. These claims include (a) non-Christians holding negative views of Christians, (b) young people holding especially negative views, and (c) the growth of these negative views over the past decade.

But before examining the claims of *UnChristian*, I would like to point out a nearly identical argument made about atheists.[6] Guy

Harrison, in his book *50 Reasons People Give for Believing in a God*, refutes belief in religion (especially Christianity) and advocates atheism. In the midst of this refutation, however, he writes that "atheists have an image problem." According to Harrison, atheists have the bad reputation of being "arrogant jerks" and "pompous fools," and he offers a remedy: Atheists should act nicer. "If more atheists would stop trying to win arguments and concentrate instead on offering their fellow humans a hand up from irrational beliefs, we might actually achieve the progress we need to survive in the twenty-first century." Reading this made me wonder if most religious groups think they have an image problem and that others don't truly understand them. If nothing else, maybe Harrison can write a book entitled *UnAtheist*?

A Few Holes in the Argument

Before getting into data—and it turns out there are plenty of good data on this issue—let's step back and think about the *UnChristian* argument and its implications. In sociological language, *UnChristian* claims that non-Christians hold negative stereotypes of Christians. Stereotypes can be applied on the basis of all sorts of personal characteristics, including race, gender, sexuality, physical appearance, nationality, social class, and of course, religion. Negative stereotypes attribute all sorts of bad things to different social groups, including laziness, dishonesty, greed, immorality, crime, and a lack of intelligence.

What's the appropriate response to a negative stereotype? Suppose that you were a member of a racial and ethnic group that was stereotyped as untrustworthy, and based on this stereotype banks were less willing to offer housing loans to members of your group (which, by the way, has happened and is illegal). Would you turn to your fellow group members and plead with them to act more trustworthy so that they were not discriminated against? Probably not. Instead, you would probably condemn the stereotypes and those who advance them.

Negative stereotypes are wrong and harmful, and we have words for people who hold them, words such as racist, bigot, sexist, anti-Semite, and so on. As a side note, it's interesting that there isn't a well-accepted term for prejudice against Christians, an absence that may reflect an unwillingness to condemn it. Maybe we need to come up with such a word. Any suggestions? How about "Christophobic"—an irrational fear of the Christian gospel and those who believe in it.

Just for the sake of argument, however, let's suppose that Evangelical Christians fully implemented *UnChristian*'s suggestions. That's right, all the major Evangelical leaders decided to meet in a hidden location, and after exchanging the secret handshake, they rededicated themselves to living like true Christians in order to reverse negative stereotypes. After that, they went home, and they and their churches lived as close to the Christian ideal as humanly possible. As Kinnaman and Lyons write, *"To shift our reputation, Christ followers must learn to respond to people in the way Jesus did."*[7] What would happen? Non-Christians' attitudes toward us might change little, if at all.

Negative stereotypes of Christians will probably persist, regardless of Christians' actions, for several reasons. Stereotypes, and the prejudice and discrimination that accompanies them, are not based in reality. They reflect ignorance, not an accurate description of the world, and so changing reality may have no effect on stereotypes. For example, no matter how many women perform well in college (and female students now constitute 57% of college students),[8] some people will persist in thinking that because they are women, they will not do as well academically as men. No matter how many presidents, Supreme Court justices, senators, or mayors we elect of racial minority groups, there will always be some people who think that racial minorities are less suitable for governance. No matter how much Christians act like Jesus, there will always be people who think that we don't. As shown in previous chapters, there are already many Christians acting in accord with their beliefs.

Negative stereotypes of Christians are also rooted in the media presentation of Christians. The media have strong financial incentive to highlight the ironic and unexpected about any subject, including religion. As long as we expect religious people to act morally, it will be front-page news when they do not. As a result, even if by some miracle, hundreds of millions of American Christians acted perfectly in accord with our belief systems, but just a few didn't, guess who would be on the front page? This, in turn, shapes people's (both Christians and non-Christians) perceptions of us as a group. Ironically, as Christians act morally, our immoral behavior becomes more "interesting" and "newsworthy," leading to greater emphasis of it in the media. This, in turn, results in more people viewing us as immoral. (Who knows, maybe we should act immorally to get people to stop saying that we are immoral?)

Finally, some people are not going to like Christians no matter what—regardless of how well we behave. How do we know this? Because some people don't like anyone who is different from them. In fact, this is even true if those people don't exist. In a classic sociological study, Eugene Hartley surveyed people about their attitudes toward various ethnic groups, including the fictitious groups "Danireans," "Pirraneans," and "Wallonians."[9] He found that those people who didn't like Blacks and Jews also did not like these three fictional groups. This suggests that the causes of prejudice and negative stereotypes are often located in the person holding the prejudice rather than the group receiving it.

Frankly, if some non-Christians hold negative stereotypes about Christians, perhaps we should view it as their problem and not ours. Trying to change their stereotypes by acting better seems, well, dysfunctional. In my opinion, we Christians should worry much more about our views of others than their views of us. We have control over our views—not theirs—and we are called to have a specific attitude toward others, i.e., love.

I wonder if we should take the thesis of *UnChristian* and turn it upside down. It claims that non-Christians' perceptions of Christians limits our ability to fulfill the mission of Christianity. Maybe it's the other way around. Maybe what's really limiting us is our perception—and concern—that non-Christians don't like us. If I think that someone doesn't like me, I'll probably want to pull away from that person and move toward those who do like me. Might this be happening with Christians' perceptions of non-Christians? If we expect disapproval from them, perhaps we will retreat to our churches where we can experience more positive relationships. If so, the real problem may be our concern about the stereotype rather than the stereotype itself.

So What Do They Really Think of Us?

Okay, enough argumentation, let's go to the data. Using the best data that I could find, I will examine three questions: What do people think of Christians? Have attitudes toward Christians become more negative in the past decade? Are young people especially negative toward Christians?

The first data come from a 2008 Gallup Poll that asked respondents from the general population—both Christians and non-Christians—how they felt about different religious or spiritual groups in the United States.[10] Respondents could answer that they had attitudes that were very positive, somewhat positive, neutral, somewhat negative, or very negative. I begin with this survey because it asks about a wide variety of religious groups, including Evangelical Christians, so we're able to make a range of comparisons. As shown in Figure 8.1, attitudes in the general populace toward religious groups vary considerably. Less than 12% of the respondents had negative feelings toward Methodists, Jews, Baptists, or Catholics. In contrast, more than one-third had such feelings toward Muslims, atheists, and, especially, Scientologists. Evangelicals and Fundamentalist Christians were in the middle of the range. About 1 in 4 Americans have negative feelings toward these two Christian groups, with the rest having positive or neutral feelings.

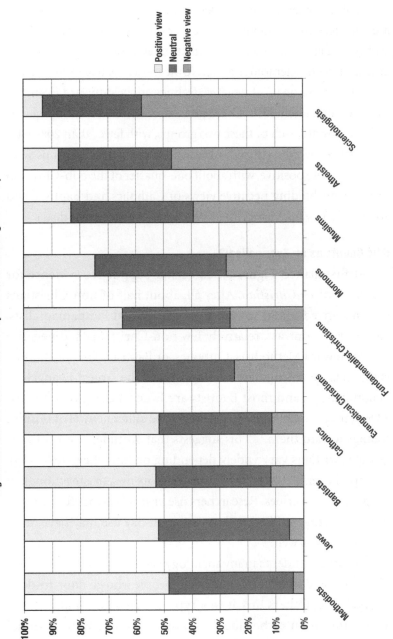

Figure 8.1: How Do You Feel about People of Different Religious Groups?

Source: Gallup 2008

Now let's focus on the attitudes of non-Christians, either those who are affiliated with a different religion or those who have no religious affiliation. Figure 8.2 describes their attitudes toward religious groups, and once again, Scientologists receive the most negative feelings. After them, however, the most negative feelings are held toward Evangelicals and Fundamentalists. One-half of non-Christians have negative attitudes toward each of these two groups, with fewer than 20% having positive feelings. Attitudes toward other Christian groups were markedly more positive, with about one-quarter of the non-Christian respondents holding negative views of Catholics and Baptists, and about 10% toward Methodists. (Who could hate a Methodist?)

Who Counts as an Evangelical?

At first glance, Figure 8.2 looks like supportive evidence for the thesis of *UnChristian*. After all, about half of non-Christians have negative feelings toward Evangelicals and Fundamentalists. However, in contrast, relatively few non-Christians had negative feelings toward Methodists, Catholics, or Baptists. This last finding is especially puzzling because Baptists are the largest Evangelical denomination, and most Baptists are Evangelicals. Yet somehow 74% of the non-Christian respondents had either neutral or positive feelings toward them.[11] This suggests that attitudes toward Evangelical Christians vary widely depending on how they are labeled. Perhaps the term *evangelical* prompts a more negative reaction than the people it describes. Researchers use *evangelical* to refer to a particular Christian affiliation, but its day-to-day use may have other connotations as well.

I've asked students in my sociology class to define "Evangelical Christian," and some think it refers to people who go door-to-door evangelizing. Others link it to a type of behavior—judgmental, angry, and often rather loony—rather than a denominational affiliation. If you want to read a more in-depth study of the

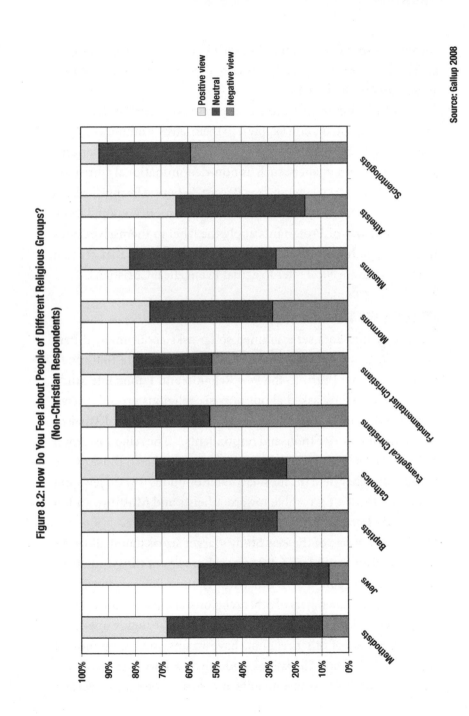

Figure 8.2: How Do You Feel about People of Different Religious Groups? (Non-Christian Respondents)

Source: Gallup 2008

meaning of being an Evangelical, check out theologians Thorsen and Wilkens' book *Everything You Know about Evangelicals Is Wrong (Well, Almost Everything).*

Another interesting feature of the term *evangelical* is that many Evangelical Christians don't apply it to themselves. Catholics think of themselves as Catholic, Jews know that they are Jewish, but Evangelicals often use other labels, such as non-denominational Christian, or a denominational label such as Baptist. Whereas Evangelicals, as defined by researchers, make up 26% of the American population, only about 10% of Protestants apply the label to themselves.[12] It's unclear, then, how much of the negative associations that are tied to the term *evangelical* refer to actual Evangelical Christians.

What Do We Think of Them?

The Gallup data set examined so far asks about many different religions, but its sample size is too small for more fine-tuned analyses, so now I turn to the Pew Religion and Public Life Study of 2007. This study asked about only six religious groups—Jews, Catholics, Evangelical Christians, Mormons, Muslims, and Atheists, but it has about three thousand respondents.[13] The religious-group attitudes of the Pew respondents were very similar to those of the Gallup Poll. They held the most favorable opinions toward Jews and Catholics, the least favorable toward atheists and Muslims, and in the middle were Evangelical Christians and Mormons.

The advantage of the Pew Study's larger size is that it allows us to consider the attitudes of different subgroups of the population, which I do in Figure 8.3. In other words, this allows us to explore what Christians, members of other religions, and people unaffiliated with religion think about each other. As shown, roughly one-third of the members of other religions have an unfavorable opinion of Muslims, Evangelical Christians, and Atheists. Forty percent of the religiously unaffiliated have an unfavorable opinion of Evangelicals,

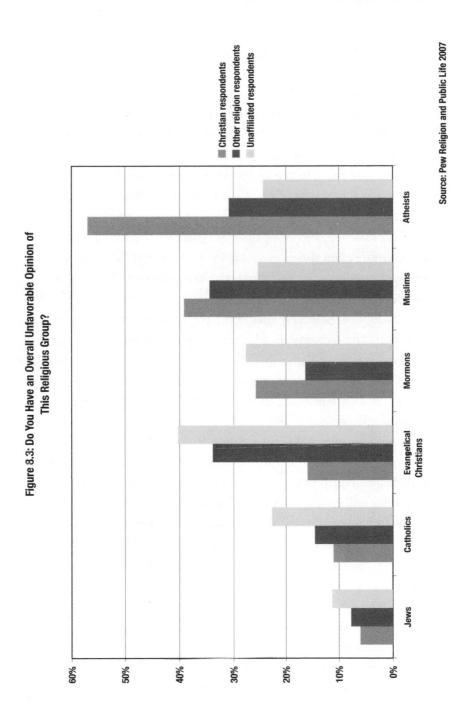

Figure 8.3: Do You Have an Overall Unfavorable Opinion of This Religious Group?

Christian respondents
Other religion respondents
Unaffiliated respondents

Source: Pew Religion and Public Life 2007

with roughly a quarter having an unfavorable opinion of Mormons, Muslims, Catholics, and atheists.[14]

Of all the groups, who has the most negative attitude? Unfortunately, it seems to be Evangelicals. Fifty-seven percent of the Christian respondents have negative attitudes toward atheists, and almost 40% of Christians think negatively of Muslims. This is ironic because Christians are called to love all people, and yet we have very negative views toward some other religious groups. Oops. On a positive note, Christians are less likely to have negative views toward Jews.

This raises an interesting question—are Christians who attend church more often also more loving to other groups? Sadly, the most frequent attendees are also those with the most negative attitudes toward Mormons, Muslims, and especially atheists. As shown in Figure 8.4, 30% of the weekly attendees have negative opinions toward Mormons and 46% toward Muslims. The most negative opinions, however, are toward atheists. Whereas 41% of the Christians who rarely attend church have negative opinions of atheists—which isn't exactly a lovefest in itself—a full 67% of weekly attendees have negative attitudes.

These findings highlight a conundrum for Evangelical Christians. Many Evangelical Christians understand Christian doctrine to include an element of exclusivity—that Christianity is true in ways that other religions are not. Yet we're called to love all people, even those who believe differently than we do. Bringing these two ideas together, Christians face the balancing act of loving non-Christians while at the same time rejecting their religious worldview. The data presented here suggest that perhaps Christians do not always make that distinction, for our attitudes toward other groups of people— not only their doctrine but the people themselves—are often negative. An interesting exception seems to be Christians' attitudes toward Jews. For whatever reason, Christians are slightly less anti-Semitic than most other groups.[15]

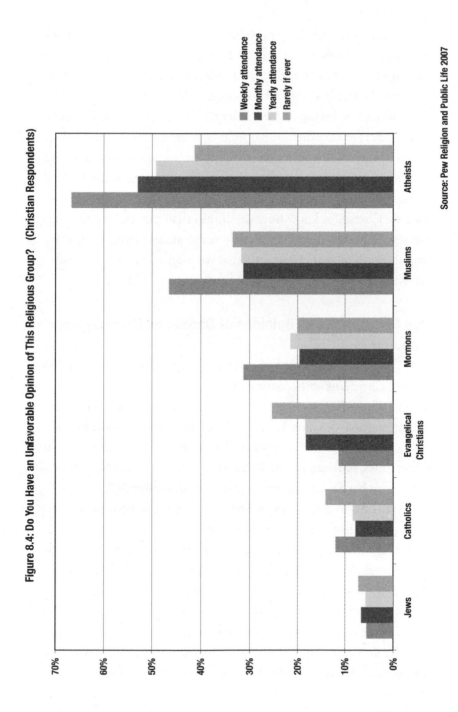

Figure 8.4: Do You Have an Unfavorable Opinion of This Religious Group? (Christian Respondents)

Source: Pew Religion and Public Life 2007

Sociologist Christian Smith interviewed Evangelical Christians nationwide about how they felt Evangelicals should respond to people of other beliefs, and they articulated eight principles. In interacting with non-believers, Christians should be faithful in their own lives, always be loving and confident, show tolerance and respect, allow others to have their own opinions, never force Christian beliefs on others, avoid disruptive confrontations, set a good example, and use voluntary persuasion through positive communication.[16] All these sound like good ideas, really good ideas in fact, and so it seems that we Christians know how we should treat others. The findings presented above, however, identify some ambivalence in how we feel about them, which suggests that we might not be as successful in living out our principles in this area as we would like.

Are Non-Christians' Opinions of Christians Growing More Negative?

The next issue to analyze is *UnChristian*'s claim that attitudes toward Christians are becoming more negative over time. This claim lends a sense of urgency to their argument, because if it's true, it may require immediate action. It turns out that the survey question analyzed in the above figures, which was collected in 2007, was also asked at other times, starting in 1990. This allows us to examine whether non-Christians have increasingly negative attitudes toward Christians. To the contrary, their attitudes toward us actually have become increasingly positive in recent years. Figure 8.5 presents attitudes toward Evangelical Christians over time among three groups—Christians, members of other religions, and the religiously unaffiliated. In the 1990s, about 70% of the religiously unaffiliated had a negative opinion of Evangelical Christians, and now only about 40% do. In the 1990s, 50 to 60% of members of other religions thought negatively of Evangelicals, but now it's down to 35%. Even among Christians, the negative views of Evangelicals has dropped from about 40% to about 20%.

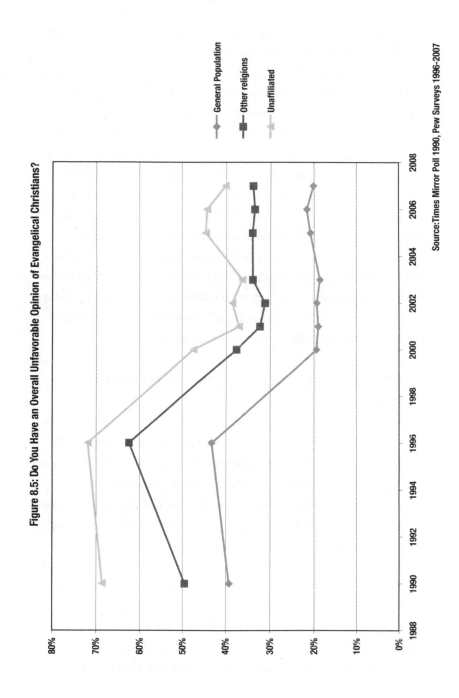

Figure 8.5: Do You Have an Overall Unfavorable Opinion of Evangelical Christians?

Source: Times Mirror Poll 1990, Pew Surveys 1996-2007

General Population

Other religions

Unaffiliated

This increasingly positive view of Evangelicals raises the question of why. One possibility, and this is speculation on my part, is based on the observation that the 1990s were a time of increased religious disaffiliation, and so perhaps the religious disaffiliation of that time shared the same causes as the heightened negative attitudes toward Evangelicals. As discussed in chapter 2, the increased religious disaffiliation was probably due to Evangelicals' organizational involvement in partisan politics. That was the heyday of the Moral Majority and the Christian Coalition. But now the figureheads of Evangelical Christianity are much less political, for example, Rick Warren, and the Willow Creek Association. So quite possibly, non-Christians (and Christians as well) think more favorably of Evangelical Christianity now because they are much less political as a group. If so, then an effective way to lessen negative public opinion of Evangelicals would be to not align our churches and denominations with specific political parties or candidates.

What About the Attitudes of the Young? Yet Another Surprise!

A final claim in *UnChristian* that I examine is that young people are particularly hostile toward Christianity. Now, it so happens that I am writing this on my forty-seventh birthday, and so how people change with age is very much on my mind. (I seem to be getting increasingly absentminded—but that may just be because I'm a professor.) To examine differences in attitudes toward religious groups in relation to age, I returned to the 2007 Pew Study, and I divided the non-Christian respondents (i.e., members of other religions and the religiously unaffiliated) into three age groups: 18–29, 30–49, and 50+. I then calculated the attitudes-toward-religions of each age group, and as shown in Figure 8.6, there are a lot of differences. Young non-Christians have the most negative views of some religious groups, including Jews, Catholics, and Mormons. However, when it

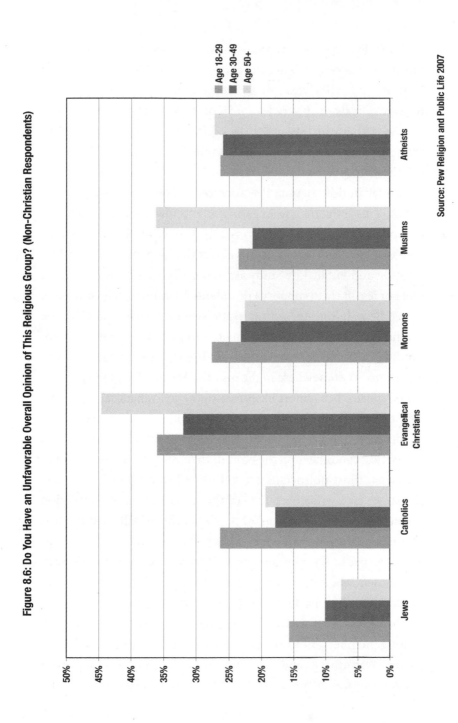

Figure 8.6: Do You Have an Unfavorable Overall Opinion of This Religious Group? (Non-Christian Respondents)

Age 18-29
Age 30-49
Age 50+

Source: Pew Religion and Public Life 2007

comes to Evangelical Christians, it is the oldest respondents, and not the youngest, who are the most negative. Forty-five percent of those over fifty years of age report an unfavorable opinion of Evangelicals, compared to 36% of young people and 32% of people in their thirties and forties.[17] It appears that to the extent that Evangelicals have an image problem, it's among older folks, not the young.

So far in this chapter, I've analyzed survey questions that ask respondents about their feelings or opinions toward specific religious groups. Another approach is to ask them how someone else's religion would affect their decisions about that person. The 2007 Pew Religion and Public Life Study asked respondents if they would be more or less likely to support a presidential candidate who professed a specific religion. According to the survey, Jewish and Catholic candidates would receive the most support, atheist and Muslim candidates would receive the least support, and Evangelicals and Mormons are somewhere in the middle. About 20% of the respondents reported being more likely to support an Evangelical candidate, 20% reported being less likely, and 60% said it would make no difference. This pattern highlights the very real discrimination faced by political candidates on the basis of their religion. It's no surprise, then, that most politicians are Mainline Protestant, Catholic, or Jewish. In fact, while over 15% of the American adult population is religiously unaffiliated, only 1% (six) of the members of the U.S. Congress identifies themselves as such.[18]

If we break the numbers down further, we find that respondents' own religious preference affects who they would support as president. Among the religiously unaffiliated, about one-third would be less supportive of an Evangelical or Muslim candidate. Among members of other religions, over 40% would be less supportive of an atheist candidate, and about one-third less supportive of Evangelical or Muslim candidates. The most negative attitudes,

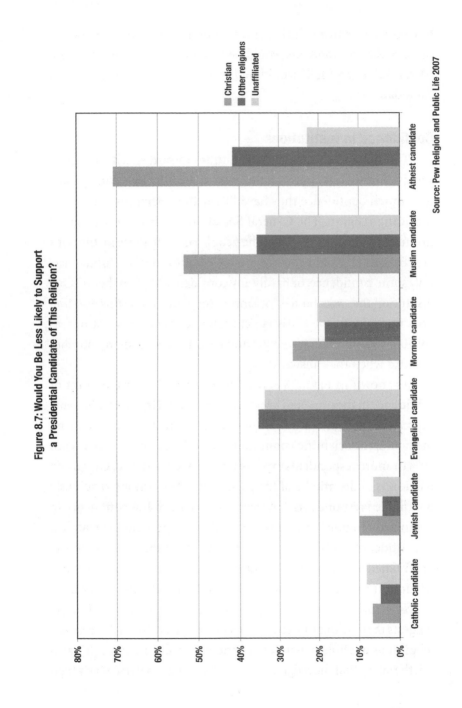

Figure 8.7: Would You Be Less Likely to Support a Presidential Candidate of This Religion?

Source: Pew Religion and Public Life 2007

however, come from Christian respondents. Seventy-one percent of Christian respondents would be less likely to vote for an atheist candidate and half would be less likely to vote for a Muslim candidate.

Confidence in Institutions

The analyses above focus on attitudes toward specific religious groups, but we can approach the issue differently by asking people how much confidence they have in various social institutions—including religion. The General Social Survey lists various social institutions and asks: "As far as the people running these institutions are concerned, would you say you have a great deal of confidence, only some confidence, or hardly any confidence at all in them?" One institution they ask about is "organized religion." While this question does not refer to the Christian church specifically, it's not unreasonable to assume that many Americans have Christian churches in mind when they answer it.

As shown in Figure 8.8, Americans have the least amount of confidence in the press and television, with only 10% of respondents expressing "a great deal" of confidence in them. At the high end are medicine, the scientific community, and the military—each with 40% or more respondents expressing lots of confidence. Organized religion is in the middle of the pack, with 24%. Among religiously unaffiliated respondents, however, there is much less confidence in organized religion, with only 8% of them expressing a great deal of confidence. This isn't too surprising, given that the religiously unaffiliated are defined, as a group, by their rejection of organized religion. It would be like asking Boston Red Sox fans if they liked the New York Yankees (which, by the way, we don't). This finding suggests that the unaffiliated may react negatively toward organized religion as a whole, regardless of the particular religion. It's also worth noting that the religiously unaffiliated have a particularly high

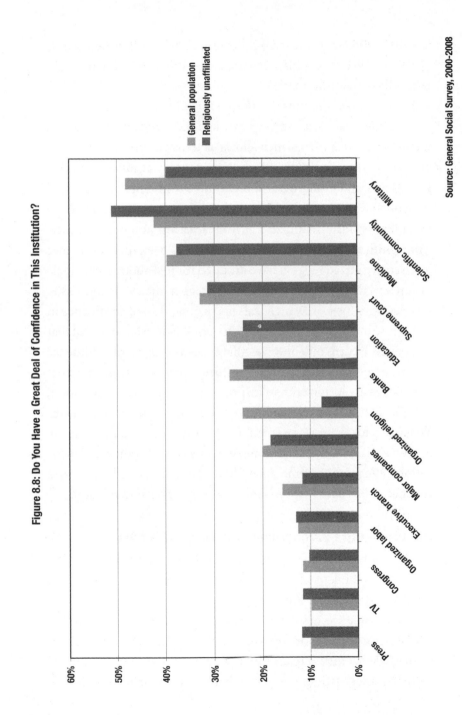

Figure 8.8: Do You Have a Great Deal of Confidence in This Institution?

General population
Religiously unaffiliated

Military
Scientific community
Medicine
Supreme Court
Education
Banks
Organized religion
Major companies
Executive branch
Organized labor
Congress
TV
Press

60%   50%   40%   30%   20%   10%   0%

Source: General Social Survey, 2000-2008

level of confidence in the scientific community—51%. Whereas only 42% of the general population has great confidence in it. This might reflect the religiously unaffiliated turning to science—having "faith" in it—to address questions answered for others by religion.

The General Social Survey has asked this question about social institutions since 1973, which allows us to track confidence in religion over time. Currently, Black Protestants, Catholics, Mainline Protestants, and Evangelicals have the most confidence in organized religion; Jews and members of other religions have less confidence; and the religiously unaffiliated have the least amount of confidence. The significant trend over time, however, has been that confidence levels in organized religion have dropped for just about every single group, and the drops were particularly steep in the 1970s and 1980s. For example, 39% of Evangelicals had a great deal of confidence in the 1970s, and this dropped to 30% in the 1980s and has stayed at that level since. It turns out, however, that a steady erosion of confidence has occurred with other social institutions as well, suggesting that Americans are losing faith in institutions as a whole.[19] In addition, specific institutions lose credibility when they experience scandals. Watergate, for example, lessened confidence in the executive branch, and financial scandals have done the same thing for financial institutions. We might assume, then, that highly publicized sexual and other scandals have had the same effect on organized religion.

Our Inaccurate Perceptions of Others' Attitudes

Most of the books and articles that I've read on this topic ask what others think of Christians. We can take this thinking one step further, however, by asking what we *think* other people think of us. There's a whole line of social psychological research that suggests that people are affected more by what *we think* others think of us than we are by what they *actually* think of us. That is, our perceptions of their attitudes often matter more than their actual attitudes.[20]

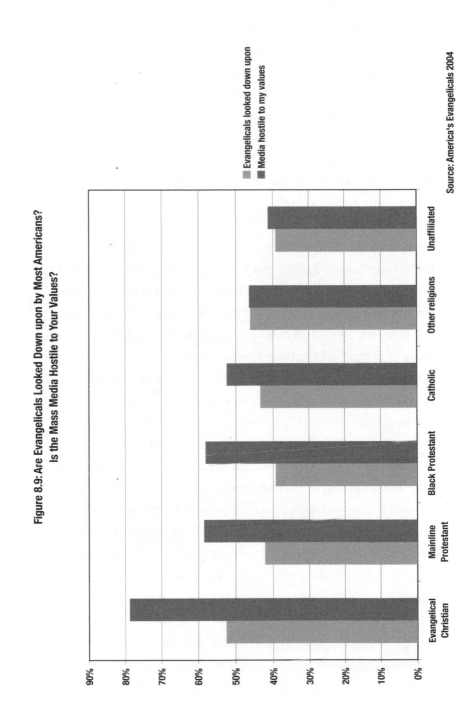

Figure 8.9: Are Evangelicals Looked Down upon by Most Americans?
Is the Mass Media Hostile to Your Values?

Evangelicals looked down upon
Media hostile to my values

Source: America's Evangelicals 2004

What, then, do Evangelicals *think* others think? Two survey questions along this line come from the 2004 America's Evangelicals Study. The respondents in this study were drawn from the general population, and they were asked whether they agreed that "Evangelical Christians are looked down upon by most Americans." As shown in Figure 8.9, 53% of Evangelicals believed that Evangelicals are looked down upon, and about 40 to 45% of the remaining respondents agreed with this statement. As you'll remember from the start of this chapter, the actual percentage of Americans who view Evangelicals negatively is closer to 20 to 25%. In other words, both Evangelicals and others think that Evangelicals are disrespected more than they are. Evangelical Christians in particular overinflate the negative opinions held about them by the general population.

Research by Christian Smith extends this finding. In interviews of Evangelical Christians, he found that the majority of them believed that Christians' values are under attack in the United States, and yet almost none of them had personally experienced hostility or discrimination as a Christian.[21] This is more evidence that we disproportionally fear negative treatment from others.

The second question in the America's Evangelicals Study asks respondents if they agree that "the mass media is hostile toward my moral and spiritual values." That is, do Evangelicals think the media is hostile to Evangelical values, do Catholics think the media is hostile to Catholic values, do the religiously unaffiliated think the media is hostile to their values, and so on. As shown in Figure 8.9, a majority of each Christian group believes that the mass media is hostile toward its values. A full 79% of Evangelicals believe this, as do 58% of other Protestants and 52% of Catholics. Among members of other religions, 46% believed that media hostility existed toward them, and 42% of the religiously unaffiliated agreed.[22]

The Real Home of Anti-Christian Attitudes

Before leaving this chapter, I want to address one more issue about perceptions of Evangelical Christians, and given the nature of my work, it's one that I'm particularly aware of: the attitudes of college faculty members. In 2007, the Institute for Jewish and Community Research surveyed the religious beliefs of over twelve hundred faculty members at various American colleges and universities.[23] As I understand it, this study was looking for anti-Semitism among faculty members, but they instead found something surprising: a strong intolerance toward Evangelical Christians.

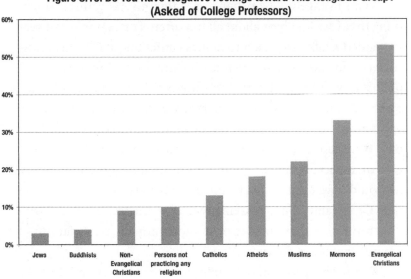

Figure 8.10: Do You Have Negative Feelings toward This Religious Group? (Asked of College Professors)

Source: Religious Beliefs and Behaviors of College Faculty, 2007

One of the questions asked faculty members if they had negative feelings toward various religious groups. As shown in Figure 8.10, over half—53%—of the faculty members reported having negative feelings toward Evangelical Christians, and this was far more than toward any other group. Twenty-two percent of faculty members had negative feelings toward Muslims, 18% toward atheists, 13% toward

205

Catholics, 9% toward non-Evangelical Christians, 4% toward Buddhists, and 3% toward Jews.[24] The study's authors concluded that "if not outright prejudice, faculty sentiment about the largest religious group in the American public borders dangerously close."

So if Evangelicals really want to find a place where they are thought poorly of, go to college. With no little irony, the faculty of America's colleges and universities rally under the banner of tolerance and diversity, but this may not be extended to all religious groups. In fact, whether intentional or not, American college campuses may have fostered climates of open hostility to Evangelical students, faculty, and staff who display their religious beliefs.

As an Evangelical Christian at a state university, this is something that I see and hear about all too often. For example, last year I attended a talk held at a humanities center about Christian missionaries in Australia. In the midst of the discussion afterward, a philosophy professor loudly exclaimed: "Christianity is a jackass religion." Then just to make sure that we all got it, he repeated it. What amazed me was that no one challenged him on it (including me). If he had said the same thing about Islam or an Eastern religion or, especially, the indigenous Aboriginal religion of Australia, he would have been beaten by the other faculty. But it was okay to slam Christianity. I'm not saying that all of the faculty agreed with him, but rather that his statement apparently wasn't so far out of bounds that it needed correction.

At a recent professional conference that I attended, I ended up in several conversations with Evangelical faculty members who felt discriminated against in their current or previous departments because of their religious beliefs. Even in my own career, I kept rather quiet about my faith before I got tenure because I didn't want to risk agitating anyone in a way that would get me fired. Instead, I waited until I got tenure before I more overtly expressed my Christian faith.

I write these stories not as an exposé about academics. After all, they are just a few stories, and there's a useful saying that the plural of anecdote is not data. Instead, my experiences in academics make it easy for me to believe in the survey findings that portray college faculty as frequently negative toward Evangelical Christianity.

CHAPTER 9

What Do We Make of It All?

This is the last chapter of the book, and I'm faced with a dilemma. I need to write a concluding chapter, because, after all, books are supposed to have them. The problem is that I usually find the concluding chapters of nonfiction books to be rather boring. Often the old adage that many of us learned in high school English class comes into play here: Say what you're going to say, say it, and then say what you've said. But it can be rather tedious to read what you've already read. Also, some authors end their books by make sweeping generalizations about how to change the future of our world (this is a favorite approach of sociologists), but these are usually far-fetched and overly general.

So here's what I'm going to do: I'll give American evangelical Christianity a report card, and then I will end the book by commissioning you to be cranky and suspicious when facing all manner of studies and statistics. As a professor, I have to take students' semester-long work and distill it into a single grade, so I'm going to take the same approach when it comes to concluding this book. The previous chapters have gone into some detail about various aspects of Evangelical Christianity in America; here I'll convert our findings into grades.

You may be thinking that this is quite an oversimplification. I am taking something as complex as religion, with its various institutions, social processes, and human experiences, filtering it through survey methods, and reducing it to single letters on a five-point grading scale. You're absolutely right; this is an oversimplification. But my hope is that it's a more accurate oversimplification than many others out there, and it might be a good way to remember and think about the more in-depth analysis already presented in this book.

On my grading scale, Evangelicals get an A in a given area if: (1) They do well compared to other groups; (2) their frequent attendees do better than less-frequent attendees; and (3) they are improving over time. They get an F if none of these are true.

You might disagree with me, of course. Looking at the same data you might assign a different grade. Well, welcome to grading. As someone who does it professionally, I know that it can be somewhat arbitrary. With that warning in mind, here are my grades:

Report Card for Evangelical Christianity in the United States

Subject	Grade	Comments
Church Growth		
Growth in American history	A	Considerable growth since the American Revolution
Growth since 1970s	B	Strong growth in absolute numbers, steady in terms of percentages
Holding on to the young	B-	Fewer young people believe, but that's the case in every generation. Possible worry about reaching those who never marry.

Subject	Grade	Comments
Retaining members	B	Lose mainly to non-affiliated, but draw from them as well
Growth by region	B	Percentages staying steady or growing in major regions, except the South
Demographics		
Gender equality	C	Christianity still a majority of women, except in leadership
Racial integration	B-	Church still predominately White, but it's been getting more diversified in recent decades.
Effect of education	A-	Beliefs and practices get stronger with more education.
Beliefs and Practices		
Orthodox beliefs	B	High levels, steady or increasing over time, perhaps due to marginal Evangelicals leaving
Practices	A-	Prayer, Bible reading, evangelism are up.
Giving	C+	Lower than we might expect. Percentage of giving has remained stable over past two decades.
Experiencing God	B+	Many experience God regularly, but some other religious groups are a bit higher.
Beliefs of young Evangelicals	B	Belief about God, Bible, and heaven remaining stable
Practices of young Evangelicals	A-	Prayer, evangelism, and probably church attendance are up in recent decades.
Sinning		
Divorce and living together	B	Relatively low rates, and less among frequent attendees, but increasing over time

211

Subject	Grade	Comments
Sex	A-	Relatively low rates of adultery, premarital sex, porn; these decrease with attendance.
Drugs	A	Low rates; decreases considerably with attendance
Everyday honesty	B	Low rates, but no consistent changes with attendance. Need better data.
Youth's behavior	B	Doing well in areas of sex, drugs, and stealing. Need to watch the fighting. Could do better with everyday honesty.
Loving Others		
Interacting with neighbors	A-	Relatively high levels, goes up with attendance
Loving attitudes	A	Selfless, empathetic toward others
Loving behaviors	C+	Could act more charitably to others, but this does increase with attendance.
Attitudes toward Blacks	D	Um, being Black is not a sin. Gets worse with attendance, but improving over time.
Attitudes toward gays	D	Not loving gays; gets worse with attendance, but improving over time
Attitudes Toward Us		
Non-Christians' attitudes toward us	B	Mixed feelings, but getting more positive over time. May not interfere much with mission.
Our attitudes toward non-Christians	C-	We like them less than they like us, yet we're called to love.
Self-concept	D+	We seem strangely ready to believe the worst about ourselves.

You know, I'm kind of enjoying this oversimplification, so let's take it a step further. That's right, after about a year of reading the scholarly literature and analyzing scores of data sets, I am distilling my evaluation of Evangelical Christianity to a single grade. I give American Evangelical Christianity a B. In other words, I would say that the church is doing well overall on the issues covered in this book. It's not excellent, because many things could be improved, but it's not average or worse, because in many ways the church is doing quite well. So there you have it: a B.[1]

What This Means for the Church

The material presented in this book has various implications. It appears that in many ways, here in America, Evangelical Christianity in particular, and Christianity as a whole, is doing a pretty good job of being the church. Well done. This is something that we American Christians can feel good about. Celebrate. Go buy yourself a dish of ice cream or give a high-five to the person sitting next to you in church next Sunday.

This positive message is very different from what we often hear from Christian leaders, teachers, and researchers. Their message can go something like this: American Christianity is rapidly dying, and Christians are immoral, disliked, and not very good at being Christians, so . . . go invite your friends to join us. Frankly, if after two millennia on Earth and several centuries in this country, Christianity is as messed up as people like to describe it, we should probably just give up. No book or conference or magazine article is going to save it now. Thankfully, this appears not to be the case, and many things are going well. When we invite others to join us in our faith, we are not asking them to jump onto a sinking ship; rather, it's a ship going at maybe three-quarters speed in mostly the right direction.

An overall positive assessment of American Christianity also means that we don't need to feel badly about being Christians. It's difficult to feel good about our faith when we are bombarded with negative messages about it. This idea struck home for me when I finished the first draft of this manuscript. I told my good friend John about what I had found, and how my findings differed from conventional wisdom. When I was done, he paused for awhile and said, somewhat cheerfully, "Oh, I guess I don't have to be embarrassed about being a Christian."

Being Honest About the Bad

Having offered a positive assessment of Evangelical Christianity, allow me now to qualify it. Another cost of the consistently negative messages that we hear about American Christianity is that we're more likely to miss the real problems when they come up. When I began this book, I didn't know what I'd find, and over the years I have been surprised, contradicted, and generally disagreed with by data so many times that I've stopped predicting how analyses will turn out. Going into chapter 6, I was feeling good about most of the analyses, and then I got to the research about Christians' attitudes toward minorities, and I was utterly dismayed. How can we love the world if we don't like the people who are different from us? These negative feelings are a real problem, and Evangelical Christianity in the United States cannot fulfill its mission if we don't like people of different races, sexualities, or belief systems. To be clear, many Evangelicals hold loving, favorable attitudes toward all others, but on average, we can do better.

I would guess that these negative attitudes toward other groups are an unintended consequence of one of Evangelical Christianity's strengths: We have forged a strong in-group identity that has allowed us not only to survive but actually to thrive in today's world.[2] Unfortunately, this Christian identity may have led us to feel less favorable toward those not in the group. So how should we change things? Beats me—I'm just a sociologist, and if you have to depend on sociology for moral guidance, you are in deep trouble. However, there are a lot of smart Christians out there who have thought a lot about these issues, and they can guide us into doing a better job of loving those who are different from us. Let's find these people and listen to them.

My opinion of the Christian church is similar to Winston Churchill's famous statement about democracy: "Democracy is the worst form of government except for all those others that have been tried." Sure the church has had its problems, but in many ways, both now and throughout history, it's been a smashing success, a great benefit for humanity. Perhaps we should say that the Christian church is the most problematic institution on Earth except for all the others that have been tried.

Will Popular Beliefs About Christianity Change? The Power of Paradigms and Incentives

Now that I've written this book, I can expect things to change, right? After all, I used the most accurate data I could find, and I tried to set aside my own personal opinions in order to present the data as simply and accurately as I could. Therefore, shouldn't I expect that if enough people read this book it will result in a more accurate, less negative public discussion of Christianity? Maybe, but maybe not. The message of this book faces an uphill battle for two reasons: paradigms and incentives.

To explain the power of paradigms, let's turn to science. A naïve view of science is that scientists base their beliefs on the best available data at any given time. Instead, what really happens, as described by Thomas Kuhn in his classic book *The Structure of Scientific Revolutions*, is that people form paradigms. A paradigm is a collection of ideas and theories about a given topic. Basically, it's somebody's view of how the world works. Paradigms have remarkable staying power because they can persist long after they have been disproved. Certainly paradigms can change—something Kuhn calls a paradigm shift—but it often takes an abundance of countering evidence, and even that may not be enough. There are countless examples of scientific paradigms that have overstayed their welcome. Classically, people believed that the sun revolved around the earth even after conclusive evidence proved otherwise. More recently, two Australian medical researchers discovered that some forms of ulcers are caused by bacteria rather than stress and anxiety, as had been previously believed. It took years and considerable energy to get people to believe them; in fact, one of them even had to drink the bacteria and give himself an ulcer.

In this book I examine paradigms about American Christianity. These paradigms include: American Christianity is rapidly declining in size; young people are leaving the church; Christians misbehave just as much as—if not more than—everyone else; Christians don't love others; and non-Christians really dislike Christians. Even if these paradigms are factually incorrect, which I think most of them are, they will have staying power because, well, they are paradigms. It will take a lot of opposing evidence to reverse them.

Let me tell you a story as an illustration. My wife and I host a weekly dinner and Bible study at our house. (She leads. I vacuum and make coffee.) About a year ago, several members started talking very animatedly about how much non-Christians hate Christians— especially Evangelical Christians. I had recently done some research on the issue (along the lines of what I've presented here in chapter 8), and so I explained to them that non-Christians' attitudes toward Christians were more charitable than we might think, and these attitudes seem to be getting more positive over time. The Bible study members found this interesting and thanked me for the information. I went into the kitchen to get some more pasta, and I ended up chatting with someone else for about twenty minutes. When I returned to the family room, the same people were saying the same things about how much non-Christians hate Christians. I looked at my hands to see if perhaps I was invisible, and I wasn't. I cleared my throat to see if I was making noise when I spoke, and I was. So why had the group—all well-educated friends—completely ignored what I had said? Paradigms don't change easily—even in the face of countering evidence. At that point I realized that nothing I could say, no matter how factual, would change their minds, so I went back to my food. With regard to this book, I hope it will change people's minds about American Christianity, but I realize that in the meantime I might spend a lot of time eating pasta.

This doesn't mean that we should not speak up when people are getting their facts wrong about Christianity. It might take a while for us to be heard, but we shouldn't give up, because paradigms can shift over time.

Another reason why we'll probably continue to hear overly negative portrayals of American Christianity is the incentives these portrayals offer. Christian authors, speakers, and leaders will sometimes pass along inaccurate, negative information in their effort to help the church. Suppose that you had a great idea for the church, and you wanted to share it with others. The first thing you would want to do is explain why people need your idea. An easy way to do that is to say that the church has been doing badly in that area so far; therefore, you're offering a remedy to a problem. For instance, do you have a new discipleship program for young people? Tell their parents about the dangers faced by their children. Do you want to get your church members to tithe more? Find some statistics about how little Christians tithe. We scare people to get them to listen to us, but the problem with this approach is that it creates scared people.

It's not just Christians who do this. The media, who want to sell more newspapers and books and commercials, attract people's attention by offering the unexpected and the ironic. With religion, this often means stories of religious people gone bad. This doesn't necessarily mean that the media is inherently biased against religion; rather, its desire for novelty leads it to sensationalize whatever it covers. Front-page stories describe planes crashing, not planes that land safely. Lead news stories tell of politicians in scandal, not those making sensible laws. Magazine covers describe corrupt businesses going bankrupt, not those making steady profits and treating their employees well. Likewise, when it comes to religion, bad news sells, and so we'll keep on reading it, seeing it, and hearing it.

Just last week a newspaper reporter interviewed me for a story about the religiously unaffiliated in New England. The reporter e-mailed me a series of questions, and I answered them with a four-page document complete with figures and graphs. The article was about the growth of religious unaffiliation in New England, and I made clear that much of the growth nationwide, and in New England, happened in the 1990s, and it has since slowed down considerably. This, however, wasn't the story that the reporter was looking for, so the article ran with quotations from others about this recent, dramatic change in the religious landscape. I have no reason to think that this reporter is biased against Christianity; rather, the reporter wanted an article that would get people's attention. This isn't always done by emphasizing accuracy.

A Call for Christians to Retract Unconditional Love

What does all this mean for you the reader? Well, if nothing else, I hope you realize the need to be more skeptical when it comes to statistics about Christianity. For reasons that I don't fully understand, statistics hold a strange power over people. Someone who is otherwise a clear thinker will readily accept something not true when it is presented as a statistic. (This is especially true for statistics presented in written form.) Statistics somehow can bypass the critical-thinking part of the brain and go straight to the "oh, that must be right" part.

Guess what? You don't have to believe all statistics! The Bible commands us to love others unconditionally, but this applies to people, not statistics. With statistics, we should be everything we shouldn't be with people—cranky, skeptical, and critical. With statistics, acceptance should be earned, not freely given.

I routinely irritate friends and family by not believing the statistics that they tell me if the statistics don't sound right. When I disagree, they sometimes respond by repeating the statistic, in case I somehow missed that it's a statistic (and therefore to be accepted at face value). I still choose not to believe it, and their reaction is often one of disbelief, as if I'm breaking some unwritten rule.

Once over a late dinner at a restaurant, I was talking with a friend, and he told me a statistic that he claimed was true that didn't sound right to me, so I told him that I didn't believe it. After repeating the statistic several times, he added the clincher: that he had read it somewhere. Now, that's the double-dog-dare of statistical presentation because, after all, who can counter it? Still, I didn't believe it, and he grew increasingly frustrated. To make a point, I borrowed the waitress' pen and wrote on the paper place mat: "The statistic is wrong." I handed it to my friend and explained that now he's "read" that the statistic is wrong, so he doesn't have to believe it. He understood my point (but he still didn't talk to me for several days).

You don't have to be a sociologist to critically evaluate data. As I described in chapter 2, *Newsweek* magazine had a cover story about the increase of religious "nones" (i.e., the unaffiliated) in the United States, and it asked provocatively whether Christian America is at an end.[3] Mark Driscoll, a well-known and often controversial pastor in Seattle, responded to the *Newsweek* story not with gloom-and-doom but with a reinterpretation. Driscoll made the case that an increased number of religiously unaffiliated Americans is not so much bad as it is clarifying. Driscoll surmises that the irreligious now face less social stigma than they have in the past, and that people who have rejected religion can now accurately identify their religious status. This, according to Driscoll, actually helps the church by reclassifying marginal, uncommitted Christians. Now, regardless of whether Driscoll is right or wrong (and I personally think he's more right than wrong), his reaction to this story illustrates that we don't have to take statistics about Christianity at face value.

We have a lot of reasons to be suspicious of social statistics. For one thing, social researchers vary in their ability, and just because someone has a PhD doesn't mean they have done the analyses correctly. When I read books or articles about Christianity that cite statistics, I routinely find basic methodological errors or other shortcomings. Maybe the sample is problematic or the survey questions are ambiguous. Sometimes the researchers misinterpret their own data. Of course, I've studied sociology and its methods for twenty years, so I see these problems pretty quickly, but that doesn't mean you need graduate training to evaluate social research. Just use your common sense. If a statistic doesn't seem right or doesn't fit with your experience, there's nothing wrong with rejecting it.

Also, researchers, like all people, have their own biases and preconceptions and these show up in their research. Ideally, in this type of work researchers should be completely neutral and simply go where the data take them, but unfortunately this is often not the case. I've aimed for this neutral approach with this book, but I don't know that I've been entirely successful. Social researchers' beliefs color our research in ways that we're not even aware of—even when we're studying "objective" facts.

Finally, we should be suspicious of social statistics because they tend to mutate when they are passed along. (I illustrated this mutation process in chapter 1.) As such, even if a researcher is highly skilled and completely neutral, his or her work might become more inaccurate with each retelling. Often this mutation results in statistics growing more dramatic over time.

As I write this concluding chapter, I have a nagging worry that you the reader won't believe that you have both the ability and the need to critically evaluate statistics. You've had a lot of training in school and day-to-day life about accepting facts from experts. Well, to make it as easy as possible, I'm going to deputize you. In the old Westerns, after a bank robbery or some other heinous act, the town sheriff would deputize town citizens, and they would ride off in a posse to catch the bad guys. I'm not going to give you a horse or a gun, but I will give you an official deputy-sociologist badge:

Cut this badge out and put it in your wallet or purse. It gives you the right to do the following with any statistic about Christianity:

- Question whether it's accurate
- Question the motives of the person writing
- Disagree with the conclusions
- Judge the statistic in light of your own experiences
- Not believe it for any reason, including just being in a cranky mood

It's official: Go forth and think for yourself about the portrayal of Christianity.

Identifying Evangelical Christians

Survey researchers typically use one of three methods for identifying Evangelical Christians. The first and most commonly used method is to measure denominational affiliation. Here researchers ask people which type of church they affiliate with. For example, the General Social Survey asks respondents: "What is your religious preference? Is it Protestant, Catholic, Jewish, some other religion, or no religion?" Those who identify themselves as Protestant are then asked: "What specific denomination is that, if any?"

Respondents' religious affiliations are classified into several categories. When possible, I have used Steensland, et al.'s (2000) RELTRAD classification method, which identifies seven religious groups in the United States: Evangelical Protestant, Mainline Protestant, Black Protestant, Catholic, Jewish, Other Religions, and Religiously Unaffiliated.

Evangelical affiliations include, but are not limited to, the following: Southern Baptist Convention; Independent Baptist in the

Evangelical Tradition; Nondenominational; Lutheran Church, Missouri Synod; Presbyterian Church in America; Assemblies of God; Church of Christ; Church of the Nazarene; Free Methodist Church; and Seventh-day Adventist.

Mainline Protestants include: American Baptist Churches in USA, United Methodist Church, Evangelical Lutheran Church in America (ELCA), Presbyterian Church USA, Episcopal Church in the USA, and United Church of Christ.

Black Protestants include: National Baptist Convention, African Methodist Episcopal, Church of God in Christ, as well as African-American participants in other Baptist denominations.

Other religions include: Buddhism, Hinduism, Islam, Mormonism, Jehovah's Witnesses, Christian Science, and Unitarian-Universalist. This classification coding scheme does not imply that these other religions are similar in content; rather, there are relatively so few of their members in this country that they typically cannot be analyzed separately, and so they are grouped together into this leftover category. Also, some of the "other" religions identify themselves as Christian. As such, the definition of *Christian* used in this book includes only the Protestant and Catholic traditions. I'll leave to others the discussion of whether some of these other religions are Christian in the theological sense.

The religiously unaffiliated include atheists, agnostics, and those who have strong religious and spiritual beliefs but do not affiliate with any particular religion.

A second approach to defining Evangelicals asks respondents if they label themselves as Evangelical. For example, the 2000 General Social Survey asked respondents: When it comes to your religious identity, would you say you are a Pentecostal, Fundamentalist, Evangelical, Mainline, or Liberal Protestant, or do none of these describe you?"

A third approach asks respondents various questions about their beliefs and practices, and the research decides who is Evangelical on the basis of respondents' answers. Perhaps the best known example of this approach is used by the Barna Group. They define born-again Christians as those who say: (1) They have made a personal commitment to Jesus Christ; and (2) believe they will go to heaven because of having confessed their sins and accepted Jesus Christ as Savior. Among born-again Christians, Evangelicals are those who agree with seven more theological points: (1) Their faith is very important, (2) they have a responsibility to share their faith with non-Christians, (3) Satan exists, (4) salvation is gained through faith alone, (5) Jesus lived a sinless life, (6) the Bible is accurate in all that it teaches, and (7) God is the perfect and powerful Creator of the world. An individual must agree with all nine of these points to be labeled Evangelical.

Significantly, the Barna Group Research's definition of being born-again leaves out many Catholics and Mainline Protestants, and in some research reports, the Barna Group Research has labeled as "non-Christian" the Catholics and Mainline Protestants who do not meet the born-again criteria.[1] Furthermore, the Barna Group Research does not ask questions about affiliation, so one could be defined as an Evangelical Christian without ever attending church.

These three measurement approaches yield different findings; in fact, Hackett and Lindsay (2008) found that the estimated number of Evangelicals in the United States ranges from 5% to almost 50%, depending on which measurement approach is used. I recommend reading their article if you want to learn more about these measurement approaches and their implications for research.

APPENDIX 2

Data Sets

Here are brief descriptions of the main data sets analyzed in this book.

America's Evangelicals

The America's Evangelicals Study was collected in 2004, and it was sponsored by *Religion and Ethics Newsweekly* and *U.S. News and World Report.* Respondents, ages eighteen and over, were contacted nationwide for a telephone interview, and the final sample size was 1,610 respondents. This included an oversample of White Evangelical Christians, allowing for more in-depth analysis of this group. These data can be accessed from the American Religious Data Archive.

ARIS

The American Religious Identification Survey is a large-scale three-part study of religion in the United States. It was collected in 1990, 2001, and 2008, with the 2001 and 2008 studies replicating the earlier 1990 study, thus documenting changes over time. Respondents were selected using random-digit-dialing in the forty-eight contiguous states. Sample sizes were roughly 113,000 in 1990; 50,000 in 2001; and 54,000 in 2008, and respondents were interviewed by phone. In each interview respondents were asked the open-ended question, "What is your religion, if any?" Responses to this question are coded into a taxonomy of religious traditions and denominations. Full reports of the study's findings are available at *american-religionsurvey-aris.org.*

General Social Survey

The General Social Survey is an ongoing national survey about a wide range of social values, attitudes, and behaviors. It is collected by the National Opinion Research Center at the University of Chicago. From 1971 to 1993 it was collected annually (except for the years 1979, 1981, and 1992). Since 1994, it has been collected every other year. The General Social Survey collects a full probability sample of all English-speaking, noninstitutionalized adults over age eighteen in the United States. Starting in 2006, Spanish speakers were added to the target population. Interviews are conducted in respondents' homes, and the survey has a high response rate because it makes numerous callbacks. Sample sizes range from about 1,500 to 4,500. The data can be accessed through the Inter-University Consortium for Political and Social Research.

Monitoring the Future

Monitoring the Future is an annual study of the beliefs, attitudes, and behaviors of high school students, college students, and young adults. I've analyzed data from the annual survey of twelfth graders, which has been gathered since 1975 by the Institute for Survey Research at the University of Michigan. Each year Monitoring the Future interviews 16,000 high school seniors from 130 randomly selected public and private schools nationwide. In smaller schools, all the seniors might be interviewed; whereas, in larger schools a random or other unbiased sample is taken. The questionnaires are administered in the classroom. The data can be accessed through the Inter-University Consortium for Political and Social Research.

National Longitudinal Study of Adolescent Health

The National Longitudinal Study of Adolescent Health is a longitudinal study of American adolescents. It started with a nationally representative sample of seventh to twelfth graders sampled in 1994 to 1995, and they have been interviewed several times since. The initial sample was taken from several hundred American high schools and middle schools. The first wave had over 20,000 respondents, and Waves 2 through 4 have had about 15,000 respondents. Surveys were collected both in the classroom and at home. Direct inquiries about the data to the Carolina Population Center at the University of North Carolina, Chapel Hill.

National Survey of Family Growth (2002)

The National Survey of Family Growth, Cycle VI, was collected in 2002 by the National Center for Health Statistics. It sampled men and women ages 15 to 44 from throughout the United States, and it interviewed a total of 12,571 respondents. The data can be accessed through the Inter-University Consortium for Political and Social Research.

National Study of Youth and Religion, Waves 1 and 2

The National Study of Youth and Religion is a nationwide study of American youth. Its first wave was collected in 2003, in which 3,370 English- and Spanish-speaking teenagers and their parents were interviewed. At the time of Wave 1, the teenagers were ages 13 to 17. Three years later, at the time of Wave 2, in 2006, the respondents were ages 16 to 20. Both data sets were collected by the University of North Carolina at Chapel Hill. These data can be accessed from the American Religious Data Archives.

Pew U.S. Religious Landscape Survey (2008)

The Pew U.S. Religious Landscape Survey is a large-scale, nationally representative study regarding religion and public life. It was collected by the Pew Foundation in 2007 with the data being published in 2008. Adult respondents were sampled from the Continental United States, and a total of 35,556 respondents were interviewed, mostly by phone. Reports on these data are available at the Web site of the Pew Forum on Religion and Public Life: *www.pewforum.org.*

Social Capital Community Survey (2006)

The Social Capital Community Survey was collected by the John F. Kennedy School of Government at Harvard University in 2006. This survey had two components: A nationwide sample of 2,741 adults and twenty-two community studies of another 9,359 adults. In this book, I analyze only the nationwide sample. Respondents were interviewed by telephone, and the data set is available from the Roper Center for Public Opinion Research.

Bivariate vs. Multivariate Analysis

This book mostly examines bivariate relationships, i.e., those between two variables, without controlling for other variables as one does in multivariate analysis. As an example, in chapter 6, I examine the relationship between religion and crime, and overall religious people are arrested less often and commit less crime than the religiously unaffiliated. This finding is open to various causal interpretations. Among them, it could be that women are more likely to be religious, women commit less crime, and so the observed association between crime and religion might only be caused by these two correlations. In statistical language, gender might make spurious the correlation between religion and crime.

Sounds simple, right? Well, as seems to always happen with issues of causality, things start to get complex. Even if the relationship between crime and religion disappears completely when controlling for gender (which it doesn't, as I show below), there could be a more elaborate causal story. Perhaps the role of women in society, especially as it relates to not committing crimes, is influenced by religious principles. If so, religion influences women's behavior, which in turn affects crime. From this perspective, the social roles associated with gender become a causally mediating variable linking religion and crime rather than being an extraneous control variable. It might explain the impact of religion rather than explaining it away.

In my analysis, I could control for gender, but why stop there? Criminologists have linked criminal behavior to many other factors, including race, social class, age, geographical region, personality characteristics, attitudes, social ties, employment, education, and past experiences with the criminal justice system. If we're to conduct a proper multivariate analysis, we should control for these other factors as well. This approach, however, considerably increases the complexity of the analysis, and one could easily write a book about religion, crime, and gender alone.

Multivariate analysis certainly has a place in academic research, and I have used it in my own scholarly publications, but for the purposes of this book, I fear that it would take the analysis far beyond the interest level of the non-academic reader. In order to examine a wide range of outcome variables, I put aside issues of causality simply to clarify the bivariate relationships of religion.

In case you were wondering, however, here is the relationship between religion and crime, controlling for gender. To simplify the presentation, I will compare Protestants to the religiously unaffiliated.

Protestant vs. Unaffiliated

Outcome	In Whole Sample	Males Only	Females Only
Arrested	9% vs. 15% *	17% vs. 22% *	3% vs. 6% *
Damaged Property	7% vs. 12% *	11% vs. 17% *	4% vs. 7% *
Stolen > $50	3% vs. 5% *	4% vs. 6% *	2% vs. 3% *
Hurt Someone in Fight	5% vs. 7% *	10% vs. 10%	2% vs. 3% *

Difference is statistically significant at p = .05. Data from Wave 3 of Add Health.

APPENDIX 4

Statistical Significance

Statistical inference is a key feature of survey research, for it allows us to know what kinds of conclusions we can make about a population of people simply by studying a sample of them.

Here's an example: Suppose we want to predict who will win the next presidential election. We could interview every single American and ask them if they will vote, and if so, who will they vote for? This would give us a reasonably accurate prediction (to the extent that people know ahead of time for whom they will vote), but it would take a lot of money and time. Instead, we would probably draw a sample of Americans. Supposing that we took a random or near-random sample, statistical inference tells us how certain we can be that our sample reflects the population as a whole. Generally speaking, assuming appropriate sampling procedures, larger samples do an overall better job of representing the population than do smaller samples.

With regard to this book, issues of statistical inference come up most acutely in comparisons of different religious groups. For example, Figure 6.1 reports that those Evangelical Christians who have ever been married are less likely to have been divorced than the religiously unaffiliated. This difference does exist among respondents in the General Social Survey, but does that mean that we can generalize to Americans as a whole (assuming the General Social Survey is an accurate representation of the American population)? Sociologists answer this type of question by testing whether the difference between the groups is statistically significant. As is commonly done, this means using statistical analysis to test if we're 95% sure that the differences we observe in a sample really do exist in the population. In this case, the difference in divorce rates between Evangelicals and the religiously unaffiliated is statistically significant, meaning that we can be reasonably certain that these two groups have different divorce rates in the American population.

It's not entirely clear what is the best way to present statistical significance tests in a book like this, which is aimed at a general audience. If I were writing for fellow sociologists, I would report all significance tests for each analysis, but this would create dozens and dozens of tables just crawling with coefficients, standard errors, and z-scores. Instead, I will present a table summarizing key significance tests on my Web site, so if you are interested, you can check it out at *brewright.com*.

NOTES

CHAPTER 1

1. The concept of statistics mutating is discussed in persuasive detail in Best, 2001.
2. One day in class, I asked my students to write down what they thought *Evangelicals* meant, and about one-third of them thought it meant something along the lines of *evangelists*.
3. *http://off the map.com/live/2008/2008/07/09/only-prostitutes-rank-lower-than-evangelicals/*.
4. *http://blindbeggar.org/?p=621*.
5. *http://stevetinning.blogspot.com/2008/07/only-prostitutes-rank-lower-than.html*.
6. A long line of social research has examined the media's social construction of the news; for example, Glassner, 2002; Altheide, 2002; and Best, 2001.
7. As quoted in Sider, 2005, 23.
8. Jenkins, 2003, 165.
9. Ibid., 166.
10. People's religion is identified using self-reported religious affiliation. For example, surveys ask "What is your religion?" or "What is your religious preference?"
11. Of course, attendance measures are not without controversy, as discussed in chapter 5.
12. In the language of social research methodology, correlations can reflect causation, selection, or spurious correlation.
13. This paragraph is based on Smith, 2000, 9.

CHAPTER 2

1. As discussed later in this chapter, many religiously unaffiliated people have strong, personal religious and spiritual beliefs, so it misstates the case to refer to them as having no religion or as atheists.

2. Hout and Fischer, 2002.

3. Ibid., 188.

4. Noll, 2001, 202.

5. McDowell and Bellis, 2006.

6. *www.christianity.com/Home/Christian%20Living%20Features/11569922/.*

7. Barnes and Lowry, 2006.

8. Wicker, 2008, 50.

9. Ibid., xiii.

10. There is controversy regarding whether Mormons and Jehovah's Witnesses should be defined as Christians. I follow the lead of studies that classify them as "other religions." Some data sets allow for the separate analysis of Mormons and Jehovah's Witnesses. Others, however, classify them as Christian or Protestant, and analysis of these data sets is not able to disentangle them. Given the different coding schemes used in various studies, in some tables Mormons and Jehovah's Witnesses are grouped with Christians, and in others they are not. Given the relatively small size of these religions, this difference in classification shouldn't meaningfully alter the results presented. My references to "all Christians" can be understood as referring to Protestants and Catholics. I offer no position on whether Mormons, Jehovah's Witnesses, and other similar groups are indeed Christian or not.

11. Sometimes Protestants are divided into three groups: Liberal, Moderate, and Fundamentalist (e.g., Smith, 1990). Other studies examine self-identification with labels such as Evangelical and Fundamentalist. (e.g., Smith, 2000).

12. Steensland et al., 2000.

13. This definition is adapted from Kellstedt, et al., 1998.

14. This definition is taken from Scherer, 1998.

15. Summarized from Steensland et al., 2000.

16. To be clear, a Black Protestant in this scheme is anyone who attends a historically Black Protestant church. An African-American person at a mainline church, for example, would be classified as Mainline Protestant.

17. With seven different lines on this figure, there are a lot of data, and

so to make it easier to look at, I've presented smoothed data rather than the raw data. Smoothed data creates a function to describe the underlying trends in data over time.

18. Kosmin and Keysar, 2009, 5.
19. Smith, 1998, 89–119.
20. Greeley and Hout, 2006, 106.
21. Kelley, 1972.
22. Olsen, 2008, 55–56, 146.
23. Johnstone, 2007, 314–319.
24. Pew Forum on Religion and Public Life, 2008a, 7.
25. Ibid., 6.
26. Ibid., 52.
27. Smith, 2002.
28. Princeton Survey Research Associates International/*Newsweek* poll (June 2008).
29. Pew Forum on Religion and Public Life, 2008, 52.
30. *www.nytimes.com/2009/04/27/us/27atheist.html.*
31. This point, that the religiously unaffiliated can be religious, has been made by others. For example, Baylor University's 2006 American Piety Study Report states that "some traditional forms of faith persist" among the religiously unaffiliated, especially belief in God and prayer.
32. Kosmin and Keysar, 2008, 7.
33. This analysis uses Census data to estimate the number of American adults alive in each of these years.
34. I conducted this analysis by using General Social Survey data to determine how many respondents were in each religion during the decade of their sixteenth birthday. This is divided by the number of Americans alive during that century, as per Census data. Unfortunately, the retrospective religion question in the GSS doesn't ask about church attendance rates in youth, so I wasn't able to implement fully Steensland et al.'s coding scheme for nondenominational Christians. I therefore split the nondenominational Christians between Evangelicals and Mainline Protestants based on the proportion of each among respondents who identified their denomination.
35. There are various technical concerns regarding the sampling procedures used in the early days by Gallup. See Glenn, 1990.
36. Initially, these questions were asked solely by Gallup Polls. More recently other survey organizations have used the same questions.

When the wording is identical, I use all the responses that I can find via the Roper Center's iPoll database.

37. Bishop, 1999, 422.

38. Smith, 2000, 200.

39. They include American Heritage Ministry, Reclaiming America for Christ, and the now defunct Center for Reclaiming America for Christ, founded by Dr. James D. Kennedy.

40. *www.reclaimamericaforchrist.org.*

41. Finke and Stark, 1992, 12.

42. Ibid., 289.

43. Ibid., 22.

44. Ibid., 22–53.

45. Smith, 2000, 32.

46. Mapp Jr., 1992.

47. Noll, 2001, chapter 9.

48. Citations from Stark, 1999.

49. Berger, 1999, 2.

50. *www.foxnews.com/story/0,2933,519517,00.html.*

51. Economist Laurence Iannaccone (1994) describes the benefit of this in terms of the church's preventing free-riders.

52. The corollary to this would be that not all numerical gains are good— something that seems theoretically possible, but an unlikely interpretation given popular church-growth theories.

CHAPTER 3

1. McDowell and Bellis, 2006, 13.

2. Ibid., 11.

3. Tryggestad, 2008.

4. "Disengage," Carey, 2008; "stop attending," Powell and Kubiak, 2005; "leave the foundations of their faith"; "forsake their faith," Tse, 2006.

5. Smith, 2007.

6. Ibid., 2007.

7. Testing explanations of age-, cohort-, and period-effects requires extensive data, for ideally the data would follow multiple cohorts over time.

8. Wuthnow, 2007, 183.

9. Hout and Fischer, 2002, 167.

10. For simplicity of presentation, I divided respondents into twenty-

year groupings. Other, more in-depth analyses have used ten- and fifteen-year groupings. Also, studies vary in which years they use to divide generations.

11. Wuthnow, 2007, 54–5.
12. These failed secularization prophesies come from Stark, 1999.
13. Cited from Wicker, 2008, xiii.
14. Spencer, 2009.
15. Olson, 2008, 175.
16. Murrow, 2005, 47.
17. Skirbekk, Goujon, and Kaufmann, forthcoming.

Chapter 4

1. Kosmin and Keysar, 2009, 11.
2. Walter and Davie, 1998.
3. *www.christianitytoday.com/ct/1998/january12/8t1044.html.*
4. Mark Chaves, Summary of National Congregational Survey. *www.soc.duke.edu/natcong/index.html.*
5. Noll, 2001, 75.
6. Michael Weisskopf, *Washington Post* (February 1, 1993).
7. Figure 4.6 presents data about the general population, which includes many Evangelicals. As a result, it might actually understate the negative relationship between education and religiosity among non-evangelicals.
8. Smith, 1998.
9. This map was produced by the Glenmary Research Center.
10. Olsen, 2008, 94.
11. Ibid., 62–64.
12. Meacham, 2009.
13. Noll, 2001, 71.
14. Fischer and Hout, 2006, 198.
15. *Pew Forum on Religion and Public Life* (February 2008): 36.
16. Used with permission. Thanks, Mike!
17. *www.internetmonk.com/archive/michael-bell-how-to-stop-the-hemorrhaging-a-follow-up-to-the-pew-forum-data.*

Chapter 5

1. *www.barna.org/barna-update/article/5-barna-update/131-a-biblical-worldview-has-a-radical-effect-on-a-persons-life.*

2. *www.barna.org/barna-update/article/18-congregations/103-barnas -annual-tracking-study-shows-americans-stay-spiritually-active-but -biblical-views-wane.*

3. Barna, 2009, 49.

4. *www.barna.org/barna-update/article/12-faithspirituality/260-most-american-christians-do-not-believe-that-satan-or-the-holy-spirit-exist.*

5. *www.cbn.com/cbnnews/us/2009/June/Do-You-Know-Your-Bible-Many-Christians-Dont/.*

6. The Christian Reformation spurred reading education. The historian James Bowen estimates early-sixteenth-century literacy rates in England to have been less than 1%, but by the start of the seventeenth century, it was closer to 50% (Kendall, 2008).

7. Christian Smith (1998) covers similar issues as above, and he finds Evangelicals high on Orthodox beliefs. He characterizes them as "thriving."

8. *www.anevangelicalmanifesto.com.*

9. Barna, 2005, 48–49.

10. For a summary of this debate, see Walsh, 1998.

11. Hadaway, Marler, and Chaves, 1998.

12. Fischer and Hout, 2006, 191.

13. Even this assumption is not without question. Studies of time-use diaries suggest the possibility that over-reporting of church attendance is increasing with time. See Walsh, 1998, for a summary of these studies.

14. Pew U.S. Religious Landscape Survey, 2008.

15. Wicker, 2008, 135.

16. Smith and Emerson, 2008.

17. Ibid., 11.

18. Ibid., 57–99.

19. McDowell and Bellis, 2006, 19.

20. Ibid., 27.

21. Ibid., 18.

22. Barna, 2005, 7.

23. Ibid., 8.

24. Ibid., 13.

25. Ibid., 20.

26. Wuthnow, 2007, 260.

Chapter 6

1. *brewright.blogspot.com/2006/11/statistics-about-christianity.html.*
2. Certainly *Digg.com* readers are not representative of the general population. I would guess that they are younger, have more men, and are more computer-savvy. This group is probably less religious than the general population, but not so dramatically as to explain the different response to these stories.
3. These data are from the General Social Survey.
4. Ellison, Barkowski, and Anderson, 1999; Ellison, 2001.
5. I wonder if the reverse is true, for Christians are raised with a tradition of confessing sins, and so they might actually be more, rather than less, likely to admit wrongs.
6. In rare cases this might reflect a respondent remarrying soon after a divorce.
7. Regnerus, 2007, 181.
8. Ibid., 159–160.
9. Salmon, 2009.
10. Hirschi and Stark, 1969.
11. The National Comorbidity study also included a question about prescription drug abuse, asking respondents if they had used prescription drugs such as tranquilizers, stimulants, and painkillers without the recommendation of a health professional. The responses to this question were nearly identical to those of hard drugs.
12. This is a good place for me to restate that this book only describes differences between religious affiliations, and it makes no effort to explain these differences. In this analysis, for example, other studies have found that women and older people are both more likely to attend church and less likely to abuse drugs. So these observed differences might simply reflect differences in who attends church. Alternately, churches' teachings on this issue might be most effective with women and the elderly, in part because they are the least prone to it. Or perhaps churches attract more women and the elderly because churches teach more normative behavior. Finally, church teaching could reduce rates of substance abuse. Testing these mechanisms is possible but complicated, and is beyond the scope of this book.
13. Burkett and White, 1974.
14. Well, right off the bat, this question illustrates why sociologists use vignette questions, because they allow us to use situations that we couldn't ethically produce ourselves. You wouldn't believe how

much trouble we get into when we run over pedestrians just to collect data.

CHAPTER 7

1. Liberation theology, for example, is a movement in Latin American Catholicism that focuses on empowering people economically; in fact, it holds that one's very salvation is inseparable from the struggle for economic social justice. Cousineau, 1998.

2. The actual question has *one* as the warmest feelings and *eight* as the coolest, but I reverse-coded the scale to make it more intuitive.

3. There is also a question about marrying a White person, but consistently few of the White respondents opposed it.

4. The sample size for Jews and Other Religions were quite small in 2002 and 2004, thus we should use caution in interpreting these four data points.

5. I use Wave 2 data here rather than Wave 1, because the older respondents, ages 16–21, are more likely to make their own decisions about charitable involvement.

CHAPTER 8

1. Kinnaman and Lyons, 2007, 25.

2. Ibid., 26.

3. Ibid., 29.

4. Ibid., 11.

5. Barna, 2009, xii.

6. Harrison, 2008, 153–160.

7. Kinnaman and Lyons, 2007, 206.

8. *www.usatoday.com/news/education/2005–10–19-male-college-cover_x .htm.*

9. Hartly and Mintz, 1946.

10. Each religious group has some respondents who are not familiar with it, and so they might not express an attitude toward that group. I drop these "don't know" respondents from my analyses in this chapter.

11. Baptists in the Evangelical tradition include the Southern Baptist Convention, Baptist Missionary Association, Free Will Baptists, and the General Association of Regular Baptists. According to the Pew Landscape Study (2008a), 94% of Baptists are either Evangelicals or in Historically Black churches.

12. As measured in the 2000 General Social Survey.

13. The study allows respondents who have heard of the religion to answer that they "can't rate" it, which I interpret to be a midpoint, neutral response.

14. As discussed in chapter 2, religious disaffiliation is not synonymous with atheism.

15. As a qualification, it's worth noting that these survey questions ask about groups of people rather than specific individuals, and so they may be capturing attitudes toward the defining features of those groups, such as their doctrinal beliefs. Possibly Christians might act very differently toward individual group members. Still, having negative attitudes toward any group would work against warm, positive interactions with them.

16. Smith, 2000, 37–48.

17. These differences are close to statistical significance, but not quite. Since I'm selecting only the non-Christians, the sample size is rather small, leading to diminished statistical power. I replicated the analysis using the larger Social Capital data, and found the same pattern of findings, with the oldest respondents having significantly less favorable attitudes toward Evangelicals.

18. *newsweek.washingtonpost.com/onfaith/faithfacts/2007/01/religious_affiliation_on_capit.html.*

19. Hoffman, 1998.

20. Sociologists have developed an entire school of thought—Symbolic Interactionism—based on this assumption.

21. Smith, 2000, 70.

22. An interesting issue is with regard to whether the secular media is actually biased against some religious groups, such as Evangelicals. I couldn't find any definitive studies, and perhaps the best summary of the literature states that religious leaders think yes and journalists think no (Hill, et al., 2001).

23. Tobin and Weinberg, 2007.

24. Faculty members' negative attitudes toward Evangelical Christians were especially pronounced when it came to the topic of politics. Seventy-one percent of the faculty respondents agreed that the country would be better off if Christian Fundamentalists kept their religious beliefs out of politics; in contrast, only 38% agreed with the same statement about Muslims.

CHAPTER 9

1. This single grade is reminiscent of a story in *The Hitchhiker's Guide*

to the Galaxy. It tells of a computer created to "answer the ultimate question of life, the universe, and everything," and the answer it came up with was 42. This required building an even bigger machine, Earth, to figure out what the question was. Similarly, Christians too would benefit from thinking more about which questions to ask in evaluating ourselves.

2. See Smith, 1998.
3. *www.foxnews.com/story/0,2933,519517,00.html.*

APPENDIX 1

1. See *brewright.blogspot.com/2006/11/statistics-about-christianity.html* for a discussion of this point.

REFERENCES

Altheide, David L. 2002. *Creating Fear: News and the Construction of Crisis.* New York: Aldine de Gruyter.

Barna, George. 2002. "Surprisingly Few Adults Outside of Christianity Have Positive Views of Christians." *www.barna.org/barna-update/article/5-barna-update/86-surprisingly-few-adults-outside-of-christianity-have-positive-views-of-christians.* Downloaded 10/22/09.

Barna, George. 2005. *Revolution.* Wheaton, IL: Barna.

Barna, George. 2009. *The Seven Faith Tribes: Who They Are, What They Believe, and Why They Matter.* Wheaton, IL: Barna.

Barnes, Rebecca, and Lindy Lowry. "The American Church in Crisis." *Outreach Magazine.* May/June 2006.

Baylor Religion Survey. 2006. *American Piety in the 21ˢᵗ Century: New Insights to the Depth and Complexity of Religion in the United States.* Baylor Institute for Studies of Religion.

Berger, Peter, ed. 1999. "The Desecularization of the World: A Global Overview." In *The Desecularization of the World: Resurgent Religion and World Politics.* Grand Rapids: Eerdmans.

Best, Joel. 2001. *Damned Lies and Statistics: Untangling Numbers from the Media, Politicians, and Activists.* Berkeley: University of California Press.

Bishop, George. 1999. "The Polls-Trends: Americans' Belief in God." *Public Opinion Quarterly* 63: 421–434.

Burkett, Steven, and Mervin White. 1974. "Hellfire and Delinquency: Another Look." *Journal for the Scientific Study of Religion* 13: 455–462.

Carcy, Jesse. 2008. "Faith No More." *Relevant Magazine.* May 29, 2008.

Cousineau, Madeleine R. 1998. "Preferential Option for the Poor." *Encyclo-*

pedia of Religion and Society, ed., William H. Swatos Jr. Walnut Creek, CA: Alta Mira Publications, Inc.

Ellison, Christopher G. 2001. "Religious Involvement and Domestic Violence among U.S. Couples." *Journal for the Scientific Study of Religion* 40(2): 269–286.

Ellison, Christopher G., John P. Bartkowski, and Kristin L. Anderson. 1999. "Are There Religious Variations in Domestic Violence?" *Journal of Family Issues* 20(1): 87–113.

Emerson, Michael O., and Christian Smith. 2000. *Divided by Faith: Evangelical Religion and the Problem of Race in America.* New York: Oxford University Press.

Finke, Roger, and Rodney Stark. 1992. *The Churching of America 1776–1990: Winners and Losers in Our Religious Economy.* New Brunswick, NJ: Rutgers University Press.

Fischer, Claude S., and Michael Hout. 2006. *Century of Difference: How America Changed in the Last One Hundred Years.* New York: Russell Sage Foundation.

Glassner, Barry. 2002. *The Culture of Fear: Why Americans Are Afraid of the Wrong Things.* New York: Basic Books.

Glenn, Norval D. 1990. Review of Andrew Greeley's *Religious Change in America. Public Opinion Quarterly* 54(3): 444–447.

Greeley, Andrew M., and Michael Hout. 2006. *The Truth about Conservative Christians: What They Think and What They Believe.* Chicago: University of Chicago Press.

Hadaway, C. Kirk, Penny Long Marler, and Mark Chaves. 1998. "Overreporting Church Attendance in America: Evidence that Demands the Same Verdict." *American Sociological Review* 63: 122–30.

Harrison, Guy P. 2008. *50 Reasons People Give for Believing in a God.* New York: Prometheus Books.

Hartley, Eugene L., and Alexander Mintz. 1946. "A Technique for the Study of the Dynamics of the Racial Saturation Point." *Sociometry* 9(10): 14–20.

Hill, Harvey, John Hickman, and Joel McLendon. 2001. "Cults and Sects and Doomsday Groups, Oh My: Media Treatment of Religion on the Eve of the Millennium." *Review of Religious Research* 43(1): 24–38.

Hirschi, Travis, and Rodney Stark. 1969. "Hellfire and Delinquency." *Social Problems* 17: 202–213.

Hoffman, John. 1998. "Confidence in Religious Institutions and Secularization: Trends and Implications. *Review of Religious Research* 39(4): 321–343.

Hout, Michael, and Claude S. Fischer 2002. "Explaining the Rise of Americans with No Religious Preference: Politics and Generation." *American Sociological Review* 67: 165–190.

Iannaccone, Laurence. 1994. "Why Strict Churches Are Strong." *American Journal of Sociology* 99(5): 1180–1211.

Jenkins, Philip. 2003. *The New Anti-Catholicism: The Last Acceptable Prejudice.* New York: Oxford University Press.

Johnstone, Ronald L. 2007. *Religion in Society: A Sociology of Religion,* 8th ed. Upper Saddle River, NJ: Pearson Prentice Hall.

Jones, Dale E., Sherri Doty, Clifford Grammich, James E. Horsch, Richard Houseal, Mac Lynn, John P. Marcum, Kenneth M. Sanchagrin, and Richard H. Taylor. 2002. *Religious Congregations and Membership in the United States 2000: An Enumeration by Region, State and County Based on Data Reported by 149 Religious Bodies.* Nashville, TN: Glenmary Research Center.

Kelley, Dean. 1972. *Why Conservative Churches Are Growing.* New York: Harper & Row.

Kellstedt, Lyman, John Green, James Guth, and Corwin Smidt. 1998. "Evangelicalism." In *Encyclopedia of Religion and Society,* ed., William H. Swatos Jr. Walnut Creek, CA: Altamira, 175-178.

Kendall, Gavin. 2008. "Literacy." *Encyclopedia of Children and Childhood in History and Society.* The Gale Group.

Kinnaman, David, and Gabe Lyons. 2007. *UnChristian: What a New Generation Really Thinks about Christianity . . . and Why It Matters.* Grand Rapids: Baker Books.

Kosmin, Barry A., and Ariela Keysar. 2009. *American Religious Identification Survey [ARIS 2008]: Summary Report.* Hartford: Trinity College.

Mapp, Alf J. Jr. 2003. *The Faiths of Our Fathers: What America's Founders Really Believed.* New York: Fall River Press.

McDowell, Josh, and David H. Bellis. 2006. *The Last Christian Generation.* Holiday, FL: Green Key Books.

Meacham, Jon. 2009. "The End of Christian America." *Newsweek.* April 13, 2009.

Murrow, David. 2005. *Why Men Hate Going to Church.* Nashville: Thomas Nelson.

Noll, Mark. 2001. *American Evangelical Christianity: An Introduction.* Oxford: Blackwell Publishers Ltd.

Olsen, David T. 2008. *The American Church in Crisis.* Grand Rapids: Zondervan.

Pew Forum on Religion and Public Life. 2008a. *U.S. Religious Landscape: Religious Affiliation: Diverse and Dynamic.* Washington, DC: Pew Research Center. *www.pewforum.org.*

Pew Forum on Religion and Public Life. 2008b. *U.S. Religious Landscape: Religious Beliefs and Practices: Diverse and Politically Relevant.* Washington, DC: Pew Research Center. *www.pewforum.org.*

Powell, Kara, and Krista Kubiak. 2005. "When the Pomp and Circumstance Fades: A Profile of Youth Group Kids Post-Youth-Group." *Youth Worker Journal.* Sept/Oct 2005.

Regnerus, Mark D. 2007. *Forbidden Fruit: Sex and Religion in the Lives of American Teenagers.* New York: Oxford University Press.

Salmon, Jacqueline L. 2009. "Many Women Targeted by Faith Leaders, Survey Says." *Washington Post.* September 10, 2009.

Scherer, Ross P. 1998. "Mainline Churches." In *Encyclopedia of Religion and Society,* ed., William H. Swatos Jr. Walnut Creek, CA: Altamira, 281-282.

Sider, Ronald J. 2005. *The Scandal of the Evangelical Conscience: Why Are Christians Living Just Like the Rest of the World?* Grand Rapids: Baker Books.

Skirbekk, V., A. Goujon, and Eric Kaufmann. Forthcoming. "Secularism, Fundamentalism or Catholicism?" IIASA Working Paper.

Smith, Christian. 1998. *American Evangelicalism: Embattled and Thriving.* Chicago: The University of Chicago Press.

Smith, Christian. 2000. *Christian America? What Evangelicals Really Want.* Berkeley: University of California Press.

Smith, Christian. 2007. "Evangelicals Behaving Badly With Statistics." *Books & Culture* January/February: 11.

Smith, Christian, and Michael O. Emerson. 2008. *Passing the Plate: Why American Christians Don't Give Away More Money.* New York: Oxford University Press.

Smith, Tom W. 1990. "Classifying Protestant Denominations." *Review of Religious Research* 31: 225–245.

Smith, Tom W. 2002. "Religious Diversity in America: The Emergence of Muslims, Buddhists, Hindus, and Others." *Journal for the Scientific Study of Religion* 41: 577–585.

Spencer, Michael. 2009. "The Coming Evangelical Collapse." *Christian Science Monitor.* March 10, 2009.

Stark, Rodney. 1996. *The Rise of Christianity*. Princeton, NJ: Princeton University Press.

Stark, Rodney. 1999. "Secularization, RIP." *Sociology of Religion* 60(3): 249–273.

Steensland, Brian, Jerry Z. Park, Mark D. Regnerus, Lynn D. Robinson, W. Bradford Wilcox, and Robert D. Woodberry. 2000. "The Measure of American Religion: Toward Improving the State of the Art." *Social Forces* 79(1): 291–318.

Tobin, Gary A., and Aryeh K. Wienberg. 2007. *Religious Beliefs and Behavior of College Faculty*. Volume 2. In *Profiles of the American University*. Institute for Jewish and Community Research.

Tryggestad, Erik. 2007. "Are We Losing Our Young People?" *The Christian Chronicle* 64(7): 1.

Tse, Rhonda. 2006. "U.S. Church Leaders, Youth Ministers Address Christian Youth Fallout." *The Christian Post*. January 12, 2006.

Walsh, Andrew. 1998. "Church, Lies, and Polling Data." *Religion in the News* 1(2).

Walter, Tony, and Grace Davie. 1998. "The Religiosity of Women in the Modern West." *British Journal of Sociology* 49(4): 640–669.

Wicker, Christine. 2008. *The Fall of the Evangelical Nation: The Surprising Crisis Inside the Church*. New York: HarperOne.

Wilkens, Steve, and Don Thorsen. *Everything You Know About Evangelicals Is Wrong*, forthcoming.

Wuthnow, Robert. 2007. *After the Baby Boomers: How Twenty- and Thirty-Somethings Are Shaping the Future of American Religion*. Princeton, NJ: Princeton University Press.

AFTERWORD

When I finished the first draft of my master's thesis so many years ago in graduate school, my advisor, Irving Piliavia, succinctly critiqued it: "This is neither accurate nor interesting." Since then, I have tried to make my research fit both of these objectives, and I hope this book does that. If not, I would like to know, and so I invite critiques, comments, and elaborations on any topic covered in this book. Just e-mail me at *bradley.wright@uconn.edu* or post on my blog at *www.brewright.blogspot.com*. Also, I have posted various supplementary materials on my Web site at *brewright.com*.

ABOUT THE AUTHOR

Bradley R. E. Wright (PhD, University of Wisconsin) is Associate Professor of Sociology at the University of Connecticut, where he researches American Christianity. Brad lives with his wife and two children in Storrs, Connecticut.